An Illustrated Guide
to the Medieval Wall Paintings
in the Church of Saint Mary the Virgin
at Chalgrove in the County of Oxfordshire

Second edition

Robert W Heath-Whyte

The Parochial Church Council of St. Mary's Church, Chalgrove

Fig 1. The north wall

Fig 2. The south wall

For Katie, Sophie, George, Cameron, Rufus and Flynn

©2016 PCC St. Mary's Chalgrove
Published by the Parochial Church Council of St. Mary's Church, 132 High Street, Chalgrove, Oxfordshire, OX44 7ST, UK.   www.chalgrovechurch.org

August 2016

ISBN 978-0-9544681-1-8

First edition May 2003 ISBN 0-9544681-0-4

Printed by Lynx DPM Limited, 35A Monument Business Park, Chalgrove, Oxfordshire, OX44 7RW.

The proceeds of sales of this book go to support the life and work of St. Mary's Church, Chalgrove.

Front cover Saint Mary holding the Christ child from the Jesse Tree painting on the north wall of the church.

Back cover St. Mary's Church, Chalgrove. Background pattern of six-leaved fleur-de-lys as scattered around the wall paintings.

Fig 3. Monumental brasses to the De Barentin family in the chancel floor

CONTENTS

INTRODUCTION TO THE SECOND EDITION

The walls of medieval churches were used like bill boards: they were covered in reminders of the crucial elements of Christian teaching, reinforcing the Catholic doctrines of the time. In the case of wall painting cycles, the stories were laid out like comic books, each scene emphasising a salient point.

The painted scheme at Chalgrove is a 700 year old example of this type of visual storytelling. Inevitably some of its immediacy has been lost over the years, and nowadays we have to work at it before we can begin to enjoy and appreciate it. It is a little the worse for wear, physical damage and decay have eroded and confused the images. The message is also obscure: we are no longer so familiar with the stories which would, in their day, have been familiar to all. The conventions of storytelling are foreign to us now: many of the rules and short-cuts, the traditions and modes of expression, that were used in medieval art, are lost on us.

This means we are several steps removed from the medieval experience, and we are stuck at a stage of struggling to make sense of what the pictures are about. Their impact is diminished and the subtleties of interpretation elude us. This is because we are looking at the paintings completely out of context.

This context is admirably provided in Mr Heath-Whyte's guide book. It demonstrates just how entrenched the storytelling conventions were throughout the Middle Ages, both over the centuries and across the kingdoms of the Christian world. He gives us the narratives, using the exact words, both biblical and apocryphal, with which the fourteenth century congregation would have been intimately acquainted. He shows us how the iconography was applied to all art, whatever the material, scale or setting, so we can familiarise ourselves with the content and language, both verbal and visual, of these stories.

This then takes us to a new point of departure: once the context is fully understood, we are free to explore ways in which the artists at Chalgrove found to individualise the storytelling, to breathe life into it and ensure that the impact of the message remained fresh.

Much of the communication is embedded in the actions and demeanour of the figures. The way their heads, hands, and even feet are painted can speak volumes. The villains are distinguished by being shown in profile, with caricatured, bulbous noses. Elsewhere the mere tilt of a head denotes grieving or mourning: see, for example, the group of apostles as the Virgin takes her leave of them, all with heads inclined and hands on cheeks in sorrow. There are some poignant hand gestures, where the Virgin's head is cradled as she is laid in her tomb, or where two angels gently support her by the elbows as she is airborne in the Assumption. The feet too can be expressive: the holy go barefoot, as a mark of humility. In the scene of the apostles bearing the Virgin's coffin, we get a sense of triumphant marching: the forward feet have toes lifted, while at the back it is the heel. Ethereal creatures, attendant angels, have shadowy bodies or consist only of disembodied hands and feet.

4

The language of gesture was common also to the performing arts, and this overlap with theatre would have added drama to the pictures. The gestures constitute a common language, as eloquent as mime, making the story telling more precise.

Some of the conventions might seem to us simplistic, for example the caricatured villains, but this is merely a device that provides the storyteller with a shorthand that avoids confusion: when we look at the cluster of Jews being offered healing if they convert, we can see that two of the crowd

stand out because they are turning to face forward, they must surely be those who have taken up the offer and are ready to adopt Christianity. This conjecture is reinforced when we notice that they are dressed in white and have fair hair.

As with any period of art, we cannot be certain whether our interpretations are correct, but it is generally accepted that not only gesture but also colour was used symbolically in the middle ages. It may also be unintentional, but in the betrayal scene, Christ is wearing a black halo which provides a black background just at the point where Judas' lips approach Christ's cheek, lending an aura of menace to the kiss.

We might expect such fixed iconography to produce stereotypical images, but the figures are full of individuality and emotion: we can see Christ's calm and composed face as he is condemned to death, and compare it with his wide-eyed, stricken expression in the Scourging. There is no lack of brutality in the massacre of the innocents, no lack of pathos in the descent from the cross. Now

that the world is so full of images of violence we have become inured, but all that spurting blood would once have been truly shocking.

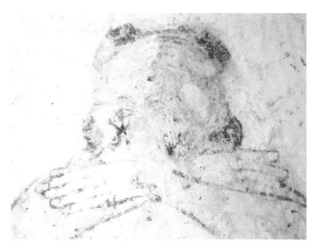

However, these stark reminders of Christ's sacrifice, set out so graphically on the north wall, are immediately counter-balanced by the assurance of the Virgin's intercession on the south wall. The two walls are painted by different hands, which highlights their opposing themes. Because the scenes are not laid out in the usual sequence, reading from top to bottom and left to right, we have initially to orientate ourselves. The encompassing message of hope and redemption is immediately apparent.

Standing in the chancel in the middle ages, one would have been immersed in the most potent doctrines of medieval Catholicism. Standing in the chancel now, one has a chance to capture some of that rich heritage. I feel sure that all those who have read Bob Heath-Whyte's book will be able to discover new meaning in the Chalgrove cycle; he has provided a key to unlock its mysteries, and the impetus for us all to delve deeply into them.

Madeleine Katkov
Conservator

INTRODUCTION TO THE FIRST EDITION

The chancel of Chalgrove church is one of the most complete works of art of the first half of the fourteenth century in England. Clearly it was built and decorated in one sustained campaign. What is more, due to the deciphering of the inscriptions above the lowest paintings on the east wall, we have the names of some at least of the donors – 'dominorum Wabor...', the Lords of Warborough, the Barentin family, who shared the Lordship of Chalgrove with the de Plessis family, whose manor house survives. The inscription referring to the Barentins is in close proximity to the picture of the Harrowing of Hell, so it could well be a plea for the souls of departed members of the family. It is placed towards the conclusion of the scenes along the north side of the life and passion of Christ. Opposite it, on the south side of the church, where the life of the Virgin is recounted, the prayer is addressed to her, and perhaps places the de Plessis family under her protection.* Sir Drew Barentin was enlarging his manor between 1300 and 1320, so he was prosperous. It is also the case that in 1317 Edward II gave the church to Thame Abbey, with the special duty to pray for the soul of his favourite, murdered five years before. This donation is the most likely trigger for the rebuilding of the Chancel. It is quite possible that the building works were scarcely complete when Edward was murdered at Berkeley in 1327. The decoration of the chancel could then have passed to the local families. The choice of subject matter reflects the emphasis of their time. The Life of Christ is represented by its beginning and its end. There are no scenes of preaching or miracles. The Virgin has featured, of course, in the first scenes of the Incarnation. The south wall picks up her story after Christ's Ascension, and is entirely Apochryphal. The Apostles visiting her empty tomb, and a rerun of the doubting Thomas theme, parallel elements in the Biblical Resurrection narratives. This choice of emphasis would be codified within two generations of the paintings at Chalgrove in the selection of the fifteen 'Mysteries' of the Rosary, an arrangement of devotional prayer under the headings of the five Joyful, five Sorrowful, and five Glorious themes of the Virgin's life. This devotional exercise was particularly fostered by the Dominicans, who had been active for a century in mission to the laity. It provided a framework for prayer suited to all occasions; it could easily be memorised, even by the unlettered.

There is only one point where I would disagree with the author of this remarkable guide book: he thinks that looking at wall paintings can be 'boring'. The nub of the matter is in their condition, but the trick is in seeing them as scattered pieces of a jig-saw puzzle of which we have lost the picture on the lid. Show us a big toe and a fish, and we deduce St. Christopher, towering to the rafters. The corner of a lily in a vase speaks of an Annunciation, the tail of a dragon and we can assume St. George. But we can only make these good guesses because we add together in our mind's eye many comparable examples. Here, for the first time, is a guide book where these close comparisons are brought together, and we can see how the pieces of the puzzle make sense. If all guide books to churches with wall paintings could be similarly illustrated, how wonderful that would be! Mr Heath-Whyte is also fortunate in being able to use sketches made of the

---

* NOTE. Sadly this interpretation was incorrect. Please see page 95 for a better understanding.

paintings when they first came to light in the 1850s. At the height of the Gothic Revival, the early fourteenth century was thought by some architects to represent the apogee of Medieval Art, so he studied these images in respectful detail. His record sometimes tells us of figures or gestures now lost. He caught the notes, you might say, but he was not a good artist, and he missed the music. If you compare his prim version of the Virgin's mantle in the Jesse Tree (Fig 12) or the Annunciation (Fig 15) with the swinging grace of the originals (Figs 13 and 16) you have the measure of what he could not convey. It is that leaping line, of ogee arch or swaying figure, that is the essence of what has been called Decorated art, and the essence of Chalgrove.

As Mr Heath-Whyte has observed, the painter would use the very irregularities of his space to suggest a couch to lean back on (Fig 44) or Calvary to climb (Fig 55). Many details of Medieval iconography are disarming in their simplicity. Christ ascends to Heaven, so we have only his feet and the bottom of his robe disappearing into a cloud (Fig 75). St. Thomas holds out in delight the girdle the Virgin has dropped down for him as she soared to heaven, and proudly displays it to the other Apostles. The line of Christ's dead arm continues, with real pathos, into the line of the weeping Virgin as she kisses his hand, (Fig 62). We are reminded of what Pietro Lorrenzetti made of the same motive at about the same time in the Lower Church of San Francesco in Assisi. The tomb of Christ with three recesses containing as many sleeping soldiers was carved at the same date to form an Easter Sepulchre in Lincoln Cathedral. It is possible a figure of the Risen Christ was once painted on the back wall at Lincoln, but at Chalgrove we have him leaping like Nijinski, with none of the sobriety Piero della Francesca brought to the subject one hundred years later.

Mr Heath-Whyte has devoted many years to deciphering the paintings at Chalgrove, their historical background, and a library of apposite comparisons. He has been supported by Mr Stephen Maynard who has generously put at his disposal and ours his MA Thesis written for the Centre for Medieval Studies at York University. This is the source for the debatable identification of the Judge as Annas rather than Pilate, (pp. 34-35) and for the renaming of the Entombment subject as the Anointing (pp. 46-47). It is not usual to have a separate scene for the anointing, and the entombment is an essential element in the cycle, so I would prefer the traditional name.

The people of Chalgrove, and the fund raising bodies who have helped them, have lavished their strength upon this church. May they now enjoy their labours in peace. But, if anything more has to be done in the future, I would be sorely tempted to explore behind one at least of the wall monuments that cover areas of the painting. Where they were fixed, the paintings will of course have gone, but there might be portions in the centre where the surface survives, and does so with freshness.

If there were a prize for the best guide book of a wall painted church, Chalgrove would be a front line contender. It will enhance the enjoyment of every visitor to the church, and remain an essential work of reference.

These paintings do not deal with quaint fables, but with the central story of the suffering, love, and the hope of mankind. The chancel of Chalgrove is an early fourteenth century prayer, articulated in a way even the illiterate villagers of the time would have understood, and which, with Mr Heath-Whyte's help, we can still understand.

Dr. Tudor-Craig, F.S.A.(Pamela Lady Wedgwood)
Sometime Chairman of the Wall Paintings Committee of the Council for the Care of Churches.
27 January 2003

AUTHOR'S PREFACE

Writing any book is not easy but writing a guide to something historical is perhaps doubly difficult in that there is always something more to research, and not enough time left to do that research before publication. The first edition of this guide contained several errors which I hope I have corrected satisfactorily in this second edition. One concerned the interpretation of the scripts written over three of the chancel paintings and the sponsorship of the chancel paintings, and while I have dealt with that fairly thoroughly, there is still more that can be researched. And, of course, while I may be sure of my interpretation there are always other experts who may have other opinions that must be respected, even if I do not agree with them. So this is definitely not the last word about the medieval wall paintings in St. Mary's Church in Chalgrove, but I hope that it fulfils my aim of making the paintings understandable to the modern viewer and that it also encourages you to find out more about the wealth of medieval art that still exists, despite the efforts of iconoclasts throughout the past seven hundred years.

There are many people who have helped me with the research for and preparation of both editions of this book and I am extremely grateful to them all. Amongst them in recent years Dr Kathryn A Smith, Professor Henry Mayr-Harting, Father Jerome Bertram, S Zakacs, Santiago Hidalgo Sanchez, Carina Garcia Codina, Giulia Lessanutti, Edward Pooley, Paul and Rachel Jacques, David Viall, and the Revd Canon Ian Cohen have all been both helpful and encouraging.

8

Thank you also to all the many institutions and individuals who have so generously given me permission to use images of artefacts in their possession and quotations from published works.

I am especially grateful to our Wall Paintings conservator, Madeleine Katkov, for writing the introduction to this second edition, but also for her enthusiasm and expertise during the Conservation and Refurbishment Project in not only preserving the chancel scheme for many more years to come, but also for uncovering and conserving the fragments of paintings from later dates which have added to the heritage of St. Mary's church. Being able to get up close to the paintings after so many years of looking at them from ground level and with Madeleine as a guide has been both a privilege and very instructive.

Margaret Molloy and Judith Bennett have both been very helpful proofreaders – and any mistakes that remain are mine alone! Dee Patel and his team at Lynx DPM have provided very practical advice on the presentation of the book.

The Heritage Lottery Fund and the Doris Field Charitable Trust have both contributed financially to the production of this book, for which I am very grateful.

And I am totally indebted to my wife, Carole, for her patience, love and encouragement, without which this book would never have happened.

Bob Heath-Whyte
Chalgrove

30 July 2016

THE SETTING

'Not more boring old wall paintings!' The comment of a teenager dragged protesting into yet another church is perhaps understandable. Looking at old wall paintings in churches and museums might be considered to be boring, especially when the paintings are badly eroded or only partially visible and so their content is obscure. The aim of this guide book is to make the wall paintings of Saint Mary's church, Chalgrove, interesting and understandable, by putting them in their context and alongside other examples of the same pictures in contemporary medieval art.

When and Who?

The Chancel of the church was extended and completely renovated and redecorated sometime during the first half of the fourteenth century.

Edward II had come to the throne in 1307 but was not the sort of man who could successfully follow in the footsteps of Edward I. Robert the Bruce inflicted a humiliating defeat on him at the Battle of Bannockburn in 1314. The next few years were marked by floods, ruined harvests, and a resulting period of serious famine in which, in 1316, even the King had difficulty in buying bread for his household. Then in 1323, his wife Queen Isabella went to France returning eventually in September 1326 with her lover Roger Mortimer, her son, the young Prince Edward (later Edward III), and an army which chased the King across the country, finally capturing him and deposing him, leading him to a grim death in Berkeley Castle in September 1327. Queen Isabella had passed through Oxford during this campaign – is it possible that the Manors at Chalgrove provided both food and soldiers to support her army? At this time Chalgrove had two overlords. The village was divided almost equally between the Barentin family, who resided in the Manor House which lay in what is now the field behind the Hardings, and the de Plessis family, whose once moated Manor House still stands in Mill Lane.

Between 1300 and 1320 Sir Drew Barentin II had a third phase of building carried out at his manor. Partly coincident with the work on the manor, during approximately 1310 to 1330, the chancel of the church of Saint Mary the Virgin, just a stone's throw from the manor, was completely rebuilt and redecorated. Who paid for this work to be done? There are two possible contenders. One is Sir Drew himself, perhaps jointly with the young Sir Edmund de Beresford, heir to the de Plessis manor. For the next five generations of the Barentin family this chancel became the family memorial chapel. The second contender is possibly King Edward II himself, though indirectly through

the Abbey of Thame. King Edward gave the living of Chalgrove to Thame Abbey in June 1317 so that the monks of Thame would say masses for the soul of Piers Gaveston, his favourite, who was murdered by the jealous barons on 19th June 1312 in a wood near Leek Wootton in Northamptonshire, Fig 4. However, the

Fig 4. The memorial to Piers Gaveston at Leek Wootton

9

identification of at least one donor, possibly Lady Barentin, in the painting of The Virgin saying farewell to the Apostles, suggests that the Barentin family were the donors.

Fig 5. The sedilia in the south wall of the Chancel

By tradition the chancel was the responsibility of the patron, in this case Thame Abbey or the Abbot of Thame, and certainly any works carried out in the chancel after 1317 would have required the approval of the Abbot. In fact in 1319 the Bishop of Lincoln issued an ordination concerning the repair and restoration of the chancel of St. Mary's.

The complete scheme of restoration would have been overseen by a master mason and would have included the construction of the sedilia (seats) and lavabo (wash basin) in the south wall of the chancel, Fig 5, which are of Italianate design, stained glass in all the windows, and it is probable that it also included a new rood screen across the chancel entrance. Even the hinges on the door in the south wall of the chancel were new, Fig 6. The distinctive flat terminals of the 'foliage' of these hinges with the full curves on the leaves date from

1350 to 1400 AD so either the hinges were not completed until after the renovation scheme or we have to date the complete renovation to some time after 1350.

Then two hundred years later came the Reformation in England. In 1535 the Bishops of the Church of England officially selected the 'Zurich' numbering of the Ten Commandments which made the second commandment 'Thou shalt not make for thyself any graven image'. As Diarmaid MacCulloch states in his book *Thomas Cranmer*, 'England was now falteringly set on the path to the destruction of images, which would be one of the most marked features of its Reformation'.

Fig 6. The 14th century hinges on the inside of the door in the south wall of the Chancel

One of the Injunctions issued by King Edward VI in 1547 decreed that 'Also, That they shall take away, utterly extinct and destroy all shrines, covering of shrines, all tables, candlesticks, trindilles or rolls of War, pictures, paintings, and all other monuments of feigned miracles, pilgrimages, Idolatory and Superstition: so that there remain no memory of the same in walls, glass windows, or elsewhere within their Churches or Houses …' and so our wall paintings were covered over with limewash and they were indeed forgotten. If the stained glass windows were not destroyed at the same time then they would certainly have been destroyed subsequently by Cromwell's Protestants during the Civil War.

Time passed and along came the Victorians and their enthusiasm for church 'restoration', and for antiquities. In June 1858, during a course of restoration work being carried out by the Revd Robert French Laurence the medieval wall paintings in the chancel were re-discovered. Being an enlightened and educated man, he recognised them for the work of art which they are and brought them to the attention of the antiquarians, and made sure that they were completely uncovered and recorded by artists, the first of whom were his own daughters.

During the next one hundred years, various techniques were developed for better preservation of wall paintings, whether Ancient Egyptian, Roman or Medieval English, and in 1967/8, 1975, 1978, 1986 and 2015/6 these techniques were used on respectively the south, east and north walls of the chancel at Chalgrove. Unfortunately, erosion caused by damp has lost some of the detail and colour of the paintings on the north wall, while the placing of two large monuments in the south wall before the re-discovery of the paintings has   destroyed two complete scenes. However,

we now have one of the most complete sets of medieval church wall paintings here in our chancel. In addition, during the 2015/6 Conservation and Refurbishment Project, more paintings from a later date were discovered on the walls of the north aisle and the south porch, and these are discussed later in this guide.

How?

It would be interesting if we knew something about the persons who painted these murals, but their identity is lost to us while their skill remains to delight us still. Professor E W Tristram in 1933 stated that 'the work belongs to the East Anglian school' and dated the paintings to be 'executed in the second quarter of the 14th century'.

The subjects and the formality of the positions and gestures of the characters in each picture are part of the rich symbolism of Christian art of this period and are discussed for each picture.

The painters would have started by dividing the wall space up with boundary lines for each picture. Such lines are still visible in some schemes in other churches but have disappeared here. Next the artists would have sketched out each scene using charcoal. It is quite likely that they would have used templates for recurring items such as the head of Mary as there is striking similarity between its execution in several places, remembering that such a template could be used to produce reverse facing images too. See Fig 8 for the stencil or template used to draw the flowers. After sketching, the artists then would have gone over the main outlines with red ochre. Then using the basic earth colours of red ochre, yellow ochre, lamp black, and white the artists would have used their eye and skill to fill in the flesh and hair colours, the drapery and drops of gore, the vitality and simple beauty that we can still see today.

The yellow ochre that was used would have been mined locally at Shotover and ground to a powder at Wheatley mill. This yellow ochre was of such excellent quality that it was exported as far away as Florence.

What and why?

Fig 7. Mary's flower symbol

A 13th century Bishop wrote 'Pictures and ornaments in churches are the lessons and scriptures of the laity ... for what writing supplies to him who can read, that does a picture supply to him who is unlearned and can only look'. But that statement belies the complexity of symbolism to be found within medieval pictures which requires the viewer to have a certain amount of knowledge in order to be able to interpret them. The medieval viewers were probably more sophisticated than we give them credit for.

There are several aspects to this symbolism, or iconography. One is the way in which the Saints point to their symbols so as to tell us who they are, for example, Saint Paul points to his sword and Saint John the Baptist points to the Lamb of God. Secondly colour is used as a 'code'. Unfortunately all the colours in our paintings have faded so what was once a dark blue on Mary's dresses is now

Fig 8. Lead stencil from Meaux Abbey, Yorkshire

black, but blue is Mary's colour and she wears it throughout our paintings until her death – more of that later. Yellow is the colour of treachery and identifies Judas for us in a nearly obliterated scene. In medieval England, though not on the continent of Europe, it was the convention that married women wore headdress, while unmarried women (virgins) did not wear headdress, and our artist uses this fact to help us to identify some of the women in the pictures. So the symbols and colours tell us a lot about the stories in each picture.

Apart from her colour code, Mary also has her own symbol of a flower. This is variously described as the lily, tulip, iris or fleur de lys and in one piece of medieval writing, the Ayenbite of Inwyt dated 1340, this symbol is described as having six leaves or petals which represent the six attributes of Mary's maidenhood as follows, 'holiness and purity of body, purity of heart, meekness, fear of God, austerity of life and steadfastness'. What a role model! The chancel of our church is of course covered in Mary's symbol, the pink six petalled flowers which are scattered above and between the other paintings, Fig 7. These would have been painted using a leaden stencil such as the one in Fig 8 which was found at Meaux Abbey in Yorkshire. This stencil produced flowers which were 70mm in diameter, the same size as the flowers on our walls.

So for the medieval viewers the wall paintings were visual reminders of well known stories and biblical truths and were an integral part of their worship and prayer. Lady Wedgwood mentions in her Introduction, the five Joyful, five Sorrowful and five Glorious mysteries of Mary as used in reciting prayer with a rosary. Of the five Joyful mysteries we have three in the wall paintings: the Annunciation, the Nativity and the Presentation in the Temple – the other two are the Visit of Mary to Elizabeth and the Finding of the boy Jesus in the Temple. Of the five Sorrowful mysteries we havefour: the Crowning with Thorns, the Scourging at the Pillar, the Carrying of the Cross and the Crucifixion: only the Agony in the Garden is missing. Of the five Glorious mysteries we have four: the Resurrection, the Ascension, the Assumption of the Blessed Virgin Mary, and the Crowning of Mary as Queen of Heaven, the fifth one being the Descent of the Holy Spirit on the Apostles.

Formal worship in a medieval church centred on the Mass and the average citizen of Chalgrove would probably have received communion once a year at Easter. For the rest of the year the highlight at each Mass was the elevation of the Host by the priest after the sacring, the prayer in which the transubstantiation was believed to take place. Just before the sacring a bell was rung so that each member of the 'congregation' could leave whatever private devotions they were making and make sure that they could see the elevated host. Just to see it was sufficient and could produce claims of miraculous results. Those with skin diseases, 'lepers', would not be allowed in the church but could look in through the squint to see the sacring. For the rest of the service individuals could make their own prayers, perhaps using their own primer, a book in which they collected their own prayers, biblical stories and pictures. Such primers were expensive but not beyond the pocket of a successful merchant or professional soldier. The poorer worshipper would recite their Pater Nosters and Ave Marias.

A great volume of the work produced by medieval artists was for the churches or about religious themes and, despite the ravages of the Reformation, some of this art is preserved for us today in a number of different mediums, in embroidery in the '*opus anglicanum*' so called because the English embroiderers were so good at it, in stained glass, in manuscript illuminations, in memorial brasses, in carved ivories, in carved wooden panels and statues, in carved stone and alabaster, in worked precious and non-precious metals making objects such as crucifixes and candlesticks, in enamelled plaques and in paintings on canvas, wood and plastered walls.

One very interesting facet of this religious art is that there appears to have been a fairly rigid format for each subject – the number of people in each scene, their position relative to each other, the direction in which they face and the position of their arms, legs and hands all seem to have been dictated by some central authority. However, rather than being laid down by religious authority like, for example, one of the controlling abbeys of the large Orders such as the Abbey of Bec, this iconography came from a school of artists in Paris, whence it appears to have spread throughout most of the western Christian church, so that whether you see the picture embroidered on a stole or in a book, in a stained glass window or in a mural, it is immediately recognizable as a particular scene, like, for instance, the Nativity or the Adoration of the Magi. Occasionally the scenes are identical except that they are mirror images – were they copied from pinhole templates which got put the wrong way round?

Our wall paintings then are not unique but where they have been damaged or have been covered over by later memorials we can at least guess quite accurately at what they are from similar scenes elsewhere. Examples of other sources for our pictures are given in the following descriptions wherever possible. The fact that these examples come from across Europe, from Italy to Norway, from Durham to Berlin, shows just how 'universal' was the language of medieval religious iconography.

THE SCHEME

At Chalgrove we are very fortunate in having a nearly complete set of early 14th century wall paintings, which are all associated in some way with the Virgin Mary, to whom the church is dedicated. The paintings can be considered under four main headings: the Incarnation and Redemption of Jesus Christ with the sequel of the Death and Triumph of His mother the Virgin Mary, the General Resurrection, and finally the individual Saints who adorn the window alcoves. The story runs from the descent of Christ from King David, in the Jesse Tree, right through to the Day of Judgement, or General Resurrection, and has been arranged so that the four moments of triumph, the Resurrection and Ascension of Christ and the Assumption and Coronation of Mary, are together on either side of the east window with Saint Peter and Saint Paul. It therefore seems most likely that the east window would have contained a stained glass representation of Christ.

Whilst the Life of Christ is a fairly common topic elsewhere, the story of the Virgin Mary is a rarity and particularly when almost complete as it is here. Surviving images of the Virgin throwing down her girdle to reassure St. Thomas are rare in this country. The Girdle itself is claimed as a great relic of Prato, 10 miles north west of Florence in Italy, and it is a popular subject in much medieval Italian art. The artists in England at this time, the first half of the 14th century, were influenced considerably by ideas coming from Florence and Siena, and the appointment of the Italian artist Bonacursus de Friscobaldi de Florencia as Rector of St. Mary's from January 1310 to May 1313 by Piers Gaveston, Earl of Cornwall and Keeper of Wallingford Castle, may have directly influenced the choice of subjects chosen for the paintings.

The selection of the Saints for the window alcoves also presents a puzzle for us. Saints Mary Magdalene and Helen are associated with the death and crucifixion of Jesus, John the Baptist and John the Evangelist are also closely associated with Jesus and Mary as are Saints Peter and Paul, but what is the link between Saints Bartholomew and Laurence and the Virgin? Perhaps it is simply that their Saints Days fall adjacent to Mary's Assumption in the calendar. It is quite possible that Saint Bartholomew was chosen, as the patron Saint of lepers, because there was leprosy in the Barentin family. We are not helped by the destruction of the stained glass windows. The window splays were clearly set aside for figures of saints and we can see this elsewhere, for example in Nassington in Northamptonshire. The adjacent windows almost certainly continued the same theme, so in each window we now see only two of what was possibly a group of four saints, two painted on the splays and two illuminated in stained glass.

Fortunately, when the paintings were re-discovered, they were sketched in great detail by Mr C A Buckler on 21st June 1859. We shall use these sketches alongside photographs and other illustrations to help in the explanation of the paintings. In the 1930s Professor E W Tristram, one of the leading authorities on wall paintings of his day, did some restoration work on the paintings and also made a number of very accurate drawings of them which he then published in his book *English Wallpaintings of the Fourteenth Century*.

During the 2015/6 renovation work our conservator, Madeleine Katkov, and her team, have made drawings of the paintings to record their present condition. We have also been very fortunate in having our paintings selected as the topic for his Master of Arts thesis by Mr Stephen Maynard, a student at the University of York Centre for Medieval Studies in 1986. I am indebted to him for a copy of his thesis and have used many of his conclusions in the following pages.

ICONOGRAPHY

Before we look at the paintings themselves, it is worth spending just a few moments to understand how the painters have given us extra information through the use of iconography. We are familiar with the icons on our computer and smart phone screens which tell us what apps we have. We may also have seen some of the portraits of famous people, painted by artists such as Rubens and Van Dyck, in which the subject stands wearing a particular form of uniform or dress. His or her hand may rest on an object, perhaps a book, a skull or a globe, and in the background there may be other items, perhaps a ship moored in a harbour or a horse. The uniform, dress, book, skull, globe, ship and horse are all devices included by the artist to tell us something about the person in the painting. This is iconography and it was used by

medieval artists just as much as by the great masters of later years.

Our artists have used several items to help us to identify the people in their paintings. They use colour, and as the Virgin Mary's colour is usually navy blue, we find her in many of our scenes wearing a cloak of a dark charcoal colour. This would have originally been blue-grey, created by mixing charcoal into white paint to make a suitable blue for Mary. Unfortunately, because the paintings were lime-washed over and then uncovered again three hundred years later, we have lost that blue tinge and so Mary's cloaks now look grey-black. The colour yellow is identified with cowardice and in one scene part of a figure wearing a yellow gown can be identified as Judas. But these colour codes do not always apply – we see other characters wearing yellow and grey-black.

Fig 9. Wimple

Then the artist uses women's medieval headdress to tell us who some of the women are. In England at the time the convention was that all married women wore headdress of some kind, whereas unmarried maidens, virgins, did not. So throughout our paintings we see that the Virgin Mary never wears a headdress. So if we see a woman wearing a headdress we know that it is not Mary but someone else. Incidentally, this was not the custom in France, Spain or Italy. The wearing of headdress also applied to widows, of course, and in two scenes we can identify widows by their

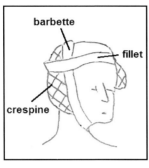

barbette

fillet

crespine

Fig 10. Barbette, fillet and crespine

headdress. There are two main types of headdress that the artists paint, the wimple, as still worn today by nuns, and the barbette, fillet and crespine, as shown in Figs 9 and 10.

Other objects that we may see are swords, which again tell us who the holder is, and crowns although sadly both of the crowns that were originally painted are now only very faintly discernible from close up.

The saints also tell us who they are by pointing to their symbols, so look out for the pointing fingers. Sometimes these are obvious and sometimes the fingers would have to be double-jointed to achieve the poses that the artist has painted! But they serve to alert us to the saints' symbols which are quite often associated with their martyrdom.

THE LIFE OF CHRIST

Being the more important of the two stories, this story is painted on the north wall of the church. Unfortunately this means that it has suffered more erosion due to sunlight and the effects of salts in the plaster than have the paintings of the story of Mary on the opposite wall.

The story starts with the Jesse Tree at the bottom left of the wall, continues with the Annunciation Window to the right of the Jesse Tree, and the Nativity and the Adoration of the Magi to the right of that. Then in the next tier up, above the Nativity is the Slaughter of the Innocents, with the Presentation in the Temple to the right. Finally the Passion story runs across the top tier from left above the Jesse Tree to right and down the right hand side of the wall, moving in to the left hand side of paintings in the east wall with the Harrowing of Hell at the bottom and rising up to the Ascension at the top. The sequence of 'reading' on all three tiers is from the west towards the east window, i.e. from left to right as you face them.

WEST
EAST

| N8 Judas p.30 | N9 The Betrayal p.32 | N10 Jesus before Annas p.34 | N11 Mocking p.36 | N12 Scourging p.38 | N13 Christ bearing the Cross p.40 | N14 Crucifixion p.42 |

| N1 Jesse Tree p.18 | N2 Gabriel — Annunciation Window p.20 | N3 Virgin Mary | N6 Slaughter of the Innocents p.26 / N4 Nativity p.22 | N7 Presentation in the Temple p.28 / N5 Adoration of the Magi p.24 | N17 St. Helen p.86 | N18 Mary Magdalene p.88 | N15 Descent from the Cross p.44 / N16 Anointing of the Body p.46 |

E3 Ascension p.52

E2 Resurrection p.50

E1 Harrowing of Hell p.48

E4 St.Peter p.80

NORTH

Fig 11. The arrangement of the paintings on the north wall and the north side of the east wall

17

Fig 12.

'A shoot shall come out from the stump of Jesse, and a branch shall grow out of his roots.' [Isaiah 11, verse 1]

'Jesus was about thirty years old when he began his work. He was the son (as was thought) of Joseph son of Heli, son of Matthat, son of Levi, son of Melchi … son of Nathan, son of David, son of Jesse … son of Seth, son of Adam, son of God.' [Luke 3, 23 - 38]

THE JESSE TREE

This is a popular local theme with the magnificent stone window-tree in Dorchester Abbey and the extraordinary tree on the painted panel ceiling of St. Helen's Church in Abingdon. Our tree has two branches of the vine forming two oval compartments indicating the descent of the infant Jesus, held by Mary, in the top oval, from King David playing his harp in the bottom oval, (St. Matthew's Gospel chapter 1, verses 1 to 17).

Other Jesse trees usually have the recumbent figure of Jesse himself lying across the bottom of the picture. In his place we have some lines of script, now indecipherable, but which is thought to be the beginning of the Lord's Prayer in Latin, 'Pater noster …' (see page 95).

The other feature to note in this scene is the figure of Mary herself, a young and really quite beautiful girl, fashionably dressed, carefully cradling her child who, with one hand resting on her neck, raises his other hand in blessing to his mother. This typifies the attitude of the artists towards the Virgin which occurs throughout our paintings, an attitude which emphasises the humanity of Mary and which is one of the artists' most touching traits (Fig 13).

Queen Mary's Psalter, now in the British Library has a more elaborate version of the Tree with three branches of the vine and Jesse lying across the bottom of the picture (Fig 14).

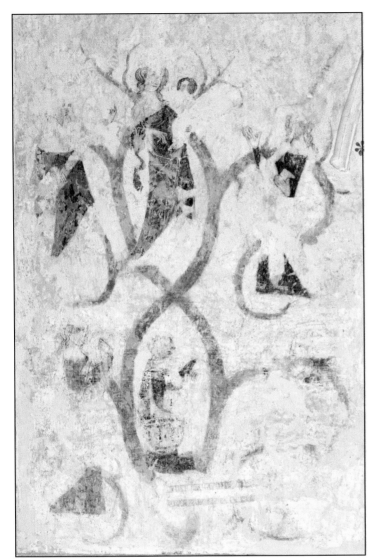

Fig 13. The Jesse Tree as it appears today. Note the two lines of script running across the bottom centre of the picture

Fig 14. The Jesse Tree from Queen Mary's Psalter, 14th C. British Library Board 09/06/2016, Royal MS 2.B. VII f.67

Fig 15.

'In the sixth month the angel Gabriel was sent by God to a town in Galilee called Nazareth, to a virgin engaged to a man whose name was Joseph, of the House of David. The virgin's name was Mary. And he came to her and said, "Greetings, favoured one! The Lord is with you". But she was much perplexed by his words and pondered what sort of greeting this might be. The angel said to her, "Do not be afraid, Mary, for you have found favour with God. And now, you will conceive in your womb and bear a son, and you will name him Jesus. He will be great, and will be called the Son of the Most High, and the Lord God will give to him the throne of his ancestor David. He will reign over the house of Jacob forever, and of his kingdom there will be no end".' [Luke 1.26 - 33]

The Annunciation is the first of the five Joyful Mysteries.

THE ANNUNCIATION WINDOW

On either side of the window we have the figures of the Archangel Gabriel (left) and Mary (right) and the paintings of stone tracery above their heads indicate that they were part of the whole window, the Annunciation being 'the window through which the Incarnation was made possible'. We do not know when our stained glass windows were destroyed, either by Edward VI's decree or by the Puritans of Cromwell's Commonwealth, but we can guess at what they contained from contemporary representations of the same scene.

From Gabriel's mouth curving down the left hand window would have been a speech banner bearing the words 'Ave Maria, gratia plena ...' (Hail Mary, full of grace ...) or as many of them as the artist could fit in. In the right hand window at the bottom would have stood a pot from which a lily grew upwards in front of Mary, the lily being her symbol. Finally in the quatrefoil shaped window at the top would have been either a dove representing the Holy Spirit or a cameo of God the Father. We can see all of these details in the two pictures opposite. Fig 18 is part of an *opus anglicanum* embroidery Orphrey of the early fourteenth century which can be seen in the Victoria and Albert Museum. Fig 19 is from a painted altarpiece by the Master of the Vyssi Brod, c.1350. What a colourful picture the whole of our annunciation window would have been !

The mediaeval theologians had solved the riddle of the virgin birth by deciding that the Holy Spirit had entered into Mary to achieve the conception through her ear when she heard the Annunciation, and so this is depicted by a small white dove flying into Mary's right ear, Figs 17, 19 and 20, and also Fig 174 on page 105.

Fig 16. The paintings as they now appear either side of the north west window

Fig 17. The head of the white dove is clearly visible in the centre of this enlargement of Mary's head

Fig 18. The Annunciation from an early 14th Century English orphrey. © Victoria and Albert Museum, London

Fig 20. Enlargement of Fig 17 showing the dove in the same position by Mary's head as in our painting, see above

Fig 19. The Annunciation altar panel by the Master of the Vyssi Brod, c.1350, now in the National Gallery in Prague. © 2016. The Print Collector/Heritage-Images/ SCALA, Florence

Fig 21.

'While they were there, the time came for her to deliver her child. And she gave birth to her firstborn son and wrapped him in bands of cloth, and laid him in a manger, because there was no place for them in the inn.' [Luke 2.6 - 7]

THE NATIVITY (Our Lady in Gesyn)

This painting has suffered most from the ravages of time and we have to refer to Mr Buckler's sketch and to other versions of this scene to understand what it probably contained.

We can just make out Mary on the left lying on a couch and some of the drapery is still visible. She is lying-in after childbirth, in medieval English 'in Gesyn'. On the right Joseph sits at the foot of the couch. The figures in the centre background are now completely gone but Buckler's sketch shows a lady, the Christ child and a disembodied hand. In the apocryphal Gospel of Pseudo-Matthew, Joseph fetched two midwives, Zelomi and Salome, to the birth of Jesus. Zelomi believed but Salome was incredulous and so her hand withered until it was cured by touching the swaddling cloth. It is possible then that the central figures shown by Buckler were Zelomi and the Christ child with the hand of Salome.

This scene is a very popular one in the medieval art of this period, and was an object of veneration, particularly by expectant mothers.

One representation of this scene can be seen in the painted wooden roof of the church in Aal in Norway, which is reproduced here (Fig 23). Nearer to Chalgrove is the stone carving discovered and now displayed in the church of St. Mary and St. Laurence in Bolsover, Derbyshire (Fig 24).

The Nativity is the third of the five Joyful Mysteries.

Fig 22. The Nativity scene as it is now

Fig 23. Scene from the painted roof of the wooden church in Aal, Norway, a copy of the original dating from c.1250 AD. The characters' positions are the same as in our painting, but there is only one midwife and the crib with baby Jesus and the ox and the ass are present

Fig 24. Our Lady in Gesyn scene in the stone carving in St. Mary and St. Laurence Church, Bolsover in Derbyshire. The midwife is in a similar position as originally in our painting

Fig 25.

'In the time of King Herod, after Jesus was born in Bethlehem of Judea, wise men from the East came to Jerusalem, asking, "Where is the child who has been born king of the Jews? For we observed his star at its rising, and have come to pay him homage". ... and there ahead of them went the star ... until it stopped over the place where the child was. When they saw that the star had stopped, they were overwhelmed with joy. On entering the house, they saw the child with Mary his mother; and they knelt down and paid him homage. Then, opening their treasure chests, they offered him gifts of gold, frankincense, and myrrh.' [Matthew 2.1 - 11]

THE ADORATION OF THE MAGI

This scene is also now almost completely lost but again we can see its composition from Mr Buckler's sketch and from contemporary works. Mary on the left holds Jesus on her lap. One of the three Kings kneels before them to present his gift, while the other two Kings stand on the right facing each other.

Comparing Buckler's sketch with the carved ivory French Diptych from the second half of the 14th century, which is now in the British Museum (Fig 27), we see that one is very nearly the mirror image of the other. The only differences are in the way the third King is holding his arms. Why this should be a mirror image of the ivory carving is not known, but may have something to do with Mary facing towards the east window in our scheme.

The same general scene is shown on the Byzantine Gold Medallion from the British Museum (Fig 28), which dates from the 6th or 7th century AD, some six or seven hundred years before our wall paintings!

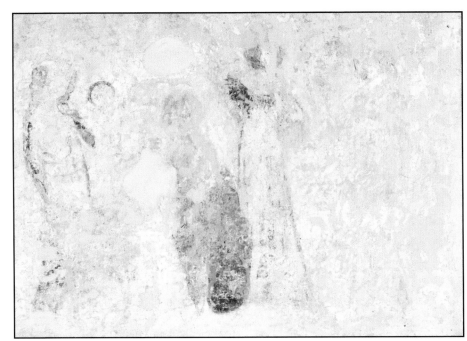

Fig 26. The Adoration of the Magi as it appears today

Fig 27. The scene from the 14th C carved ivory French Diptych. See also Fig 73 on page 51. © The Trustees of the British Museum. All rights reserved.

Fig 28. Byzantine Gold medallion. © The Trustees of the British Museum. All rights reserved.

25

Fig 29.

'When Herod saw that he had been tricked by the wise men, he was infuriated, and he sent and killed all the children in and around Bethlehem who were two years old or under, according to the time that he had learned from the wise men.' [Matthew 2.16]

THE SLAUGHTER OF THE INNOCENTS

Much of this grisly scene is missing, but it is our first introduction to the artist's partiality for showing copious gouts of blood! King Herod sits on a throne on the left facing a spear on which is impaled a baby boy, dripping blood. The spear is held by a soldier no longer visible behind whom there were possibly two other cameos, first a mother struggling with a soldier over a murdered child – she trying to pluck out one of the soldier's eyes – each of them grasping one of the child's arms, and second a distressed mother holding her dead child. This is the typical sequence for depicting this topic as is shown in the manuscript picture from the De Lisle Psalter Fig 32.

Professor Tristram's sketch from 1932 shows more detail than we can see now, Fig 30, below.

Fig 30. Professor Tristram's sketch

Fig 31. The Slaughter of the Innocents. Note the child impaled on the spear

Fig 32. The Slaughter of the Innocents from the De Lisle Psalter, c.1310, now in the British Library. Note that this is a mirror image of ours and differs in the placing of the child impaled on the spear. British Library Board 09/06/2016, Arundel 83, f.124v

Fig 33.

'When the time came for their purification according to the law of Moses, they brought him up to Jerusalem to present him to the Lord ... and they offered a sacrifice ... a pair of turtledoves or two young pigeons ... Guided by the Spirit, Simeon came into the temple; and when the parents brought in the child Jesus, to do for him what was customary under the law, Simeon took him in his arms and praised God, saying "Master, now you are dismissing your servant in peace, according to your word; for my eyes have seen your salvation ..." There was also a prophet, Anna the daughter of Phanuel, of the tribe of Asher. She was of a great age, having lived with her husband seven years after marriage, then as a widow to the age of eighty-four ... At that moment she came, and began to praise God and to speak about the child to all who were looking for the redemption of Jerusalem.' [Luke 2.22 - 38]

THE PRESENTATION IN THE TEMPLE

Of this section of four pictures of the childhood of Jesus, this painting is the best preserved. Simeon on the right of the altar stretches out his hand in blessing to Jesus, who is held out to him by Mary. Behind Mary stands Anna the prophetess, identified by the medieval headdress of barbette, fillet and crespine net (see Iconography page 15), and beside her is a second figure. We might expect this to be Joseph and, while this person might at first glance appear to be female, he clearly has a beard. Usually in this scene Joseph, or Anna, is shown carrying a basket of doves, but although there is a space where this might have been, Fig 36, of a similar shape to Anna's basket in Fig 34, it has now disappeared. The picture in the Laud manuscript (c.1380–c.1400), Fig 35, has the same layout as ours, with Anna and doves, but no Joseph.

The Presentation in the Temple is the fourth of the five Joyful Mysteries.

Fig 34. The Presentation in the Temple

Fig 35. The Presentation from the Laud Manuscript in the Bodleian Library

Fig 36. The basket shape in front of Joseph and Anna

THE PASSION OF CHRIST

The Passion story runs across the top of the north wall and appears to follow the story as told in Saint John's Gospel, chapters 13 to 19.

'After saying this Jesus was troubled in spirit, and declared, "Very truly, I tell you, one of you will betray me". … One of his disciples … asked him, "Lord, who is it?" Jesus answered, "It is the one to whom I give this piece of bread when I have dipped it in the dish". So when he had dipped the piece of bread, he gave it to Judas son of Simon Iscariot. After he received the bread, Satan entered into him. Jesus said to him, "Do quickly what you are going to do" … So after receiving the piece of bread, he immediately went out. And it was night.' [John 13, 21- 30]

JUDAS

The story starts in the west (left hand as you face it) corner with a badly damaged scene (Fig 38) of which only the right hand figure remains, headless and in yellow ochre robes facing into the corner. In all of the scenes on our walls the characters face inwards towards each other and the clue as to which way they are facing is given by the lines of their clothes. This figure then was on the right hand side of a small scene with one or perhaps a couple of other figures. C A Buckler's sketches of 1859 do not show this figure and it only really became visible during the restoration work on the north wall in 1986. Assuming that the now blank west wall above the chancel arch once held a magnificent painting of the Last Supper, (this is a wild guess on my part with no supporting evidence except that it is an obvious place for such a picture, there being such a scene in this position in the church of Strangnas in Sweden and also at Fairsteads church in Essex, Fig 37), then the mystery scene could have been either Judas receiving the silver, or Jesus' agony in the garden. However, we know that yellow is the colour of treachery and so it is probably Judas who is portrayed here receiving his silver.

The carved ivory in the French Diptych from the Soissons group (Fig 39) shows the three scenes of Judas' betrayal and the first scene matches the position of this scene here.

Fig 38. The scene on the north wall to the left of the Betrayal

Fig 37. The painted wall across the chancel arch in the church at Fairsteads in Essex. At the top Christ enters Jerusalem on a donkey, while a child in the tree cuts down branches to throw before him. Below this, the Last Supper is on the left and the Betrayal on the right. The two figures in the centre, below the tree, are part of the Betrayal scene

Fig 39. Part of the carved ivory French Soissons Diptych from the end of the 13th century showing Judas' betrayal. Note the three scenes – Judas receives the silver, left, kisses Jesus, centre, and hangs disembowelled from a tree, right. See also page 104.
© Victoria and Albert Museum, London

Fig 40.

'So Judas brought a detachment of soldiers together with police from the chief priests and the Pharisees, and they came there with lanterns and torches and weapons. Then Jesus, knowing all that was to happen to him, came forward and asked them, "Whom are you looking for?" They replied "Jesus of Nazareth". Jesus replied, "I am he"…. Then Simon Peter, who had a sword, drew it, struck the high priest's slave, and cut off his right ear. The slave's name was Malchus.' [John 18.3 - 10]

THE BETRAYAL

To the right of Judas is the scene depicting Judas' kiss of betrayal. On the left hand side we see Peter in a dark mantle with his left hand raised to stop the arrest of Jesus, while with the sword in his right hand he casually lops off the ear of Malchus, the High Priest's servant. Malchus appears to be kneeling and is much smaller than Peter, and of course there are copious gouts of blood flowing from his ear!

To the right of Peter and Malchus, Judas reaches across the front of Jesus to embrace him and plant the traitor's kiss, while Jesus stretches out his hand to cure Malchus' ear. Behind them, and to the right are other figures who are probably soldiers (there is a fist grasping the handle of a spear) and apostles. Alternatively in this position, on the extreme right hand side of the scene could have been Judas hanging from his traitor's tree with his guts spilling out, as in the carved ivory Soissons Diptych (Fig 39 and page 104).

The three central subjects of Peter and Malchus, the kiss of betrayal and the arrest of Jesus form the content of most versions of this scene. A typical manuscript version comes from the collection of canticles, hymns and the Passion of Christ, c.1280 to c.1290, Fig 42, originating from St. Augustine's at Canterbury and now owned by St. John's College, Cambridge.

Fig 41. The Betrayal

Fig 42. Picture of the Betrayal from the manuscript collection from St. Augustine's Canterbury, now owned by St. John's College, Cambridge

Fig 43.

'So the soldiers, their officer, and the Jewish police arrested Jesus and bound him. First they took him to Annas, who was the father-in-law of Caiaphas, the high priest that year.' [Mark 14.53 - 55]

JESUS BEFORE ANNAS

On the other side of the top of the window arch we see Jesus brought before Annas. I had previously thought that the 'judge' in this picture was Pilate but Stephen Maynard points out quite correctly that if the sequence of pictures follows the story narrated in the gospels then this picture must show Jesus before either Caiaphas or Annas, the latter being most likely the subject of our painting, as this incident gets more verses in John's version of the story than does the visit to Caiaphas.

Annas, seated on the window arch, wears a cap and raises his right hand in accusation, while Jesus to the right of him is held between two servants.

The comparable version of the picture, from the Gough Psalter, Fig 45, is in reverse of our version and raises once again who is the judge as it is entitled 'Christ before Caiaphas'. A similar picture in the Sarum Hours, c.1340 to c.1350, now owned by Trinity College, Dublin, is entitled 'Christ before Pilate' as was our sketch by Mr Buckler.

In Fig 44 we see for the first time the caricature of the large noses of the two men on either side of Jesus, holding him prisoner. We see this caricature in all subsequent pictures where the artist wants us to recognise the baddies. This caricature is anti-Semitic and we have to remember that when these paintings were made the Jews had been banned from England since 1290 when King Edward I issued an Edict of Expulsion. This ban remained until the 17th Century.

Fig 44. Jesus before Annas

Fig 45. 'Christ before Caiaphas' from the Gough Psalter

Fig 46.

'And the soldiers wove a crown of thorns and put it on his head, and they dressed him in a purple robe. They kept coming up to him, saying, "Hail, King of the Jews!" and striking him on the face.'
[John 19.2 - 3]

THE MOCKING BY THE SOLDIERS

Very little remains of this scene, which is of a fairly standard composition. Christ is blindfolded and stands between two people. The one on the right looks up and sticks out his tongue, while the one on the left appears to be laughing and wears a conical shaped 'Jews' hat with a very long curly point. There are in fact traces of two other people in the picture, above and 'behind' the two that we can see, with a hand apparently placing the crown of thorns on Jesus' head. Jesus' bound hands are shown in Buckler's sketch but are now barely visible.

A comparable scene in an enamelled plaque from the French Limoges workshop of Nardon Pericaud (dated circa 1520), Fig 49, shows the scene more clearly. Christ seated wears the crimson robe and crown of thorns while two people kneel to him and two others are hitting him with reeds.

The scene from the wall paintings of St. Teilo's church in Glamorgan, Fig 48, which were discovered shortly before the derelict building was demolished, and moved completely to the Welsh Folk Museum at St. Fagans near Cardiff, shows two people spitting at Jesus which is probably what the characters in our wall painting were doing.

The Crowning with Thorns is the second of the five Sorrowful Mysteries.

Fig 47. The Mocking as it appears today

Fig 49. The French enamel plaque, circa 1520 AD, from the Limoges Workshop, now in the Fitzwilliam Museum in Cambridge, clearly shows the full picture

Fig 48. The fragment of wall painting from St. Teilo's church, now in the Welsh Folk Museum

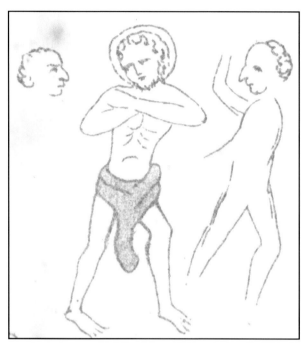

Fig 50.

'Then Pilate took Jesus and had him flogged.' [John 19.1]

THE SCOURGING OF JESUS

The next cameo scene is also composed of three figures. Again Christ is in the centre, his bound hands held across his chest, presumably tied to a vertical post of which there is no trace. He wears just a cloth around his loins and is dotted with black specks representing blood. The heads of his two assailants are visible on either side and above the one on the left can be clearly seen his two fists grasping the scourge to be brought down across Jesus' back.

The *opus anglicanum* version of this scene, now in the Victoria and Albert Museum, Fig 52, comes from the Marnhull orphrey (border) of a chasuble (sleeveless cloak worn by a priest at the eucharist) dated to the early fourteenth century, in other words contemporary with our paintings. It shows Jesus in a similar sort of stance with his head facing left forwards and wrapped around the post to which he is tied. The bespattered specks of blood are there and the two-handed method of using the scourge.

It is not clear whether or not our painting had the scourging post. There is no sign of it at all either above or below Jesus' head, and as some artists adopted the idea of placing the post behind Jesus while showing him in the same position as if he was tied to a post in front of him, as in the picture from the Gough manuscript, Fig 53, it is possible that this idea has been used here.

The Scourging at the Pillar is the third of the five Sorrowful Mysteries.

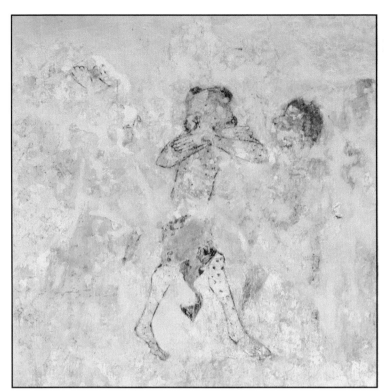

Fig 51. The Scourging - note the raised hands holding the whip top left and the drops of blood on Jesus' legs

Fig 52. Part of the *opus anglicanum* embroidered Marnhull orphrey showing the Scourging.
© Victoria and Albert Museum, London

Fig 53. The same scene from the Gough Psalter

Fig 54.

'Then he handed him over to them to be crucified. So they took Jesus; and carrying the cross by himself, he went out to what is called The Place of the Skull, which in Hebrew is called Golgotha.' [John 19.16 - 17]

CHRIST BEARING THE CROSS

In the same way as our artist has Annas leaning against the window slope to cross-examine Jesus, so in this scene he uses the rising slope of the next window to represent the hill of Calvary. A man carrying a bucket, containing presumably the hammer and nails, leads Jesus up this hill. Jesus carries the cross over his right shoulder and is followed by other figures. He looks backwards but Buckler's sketch does not show anyone behind him. In the Gough Psalter version of the picture, as shown below, Fig 56, and the photograph of the wall painting as it is today, Fig 55, we can see a soldier behind Jesus whipping him onwards. Behind him the Gough Psalter picture shows a woman in blue, the Virgin Mary, and in our wall painting there is a shadowy female figure at the left hand side which could well have been Mary.

The Carrying of the Cross is the fourth of the five Sorrowful Mysteries.

Fig 55. Christ bearing the Cross

Fig 56. Again the manuscript Gough Psalter in the Bodleian Library shows a very similar scene

41

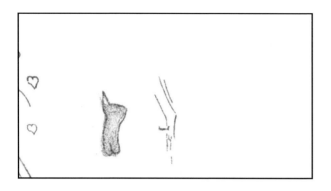

Fig 57.

'There they crucified him, and with him two others, one on either side, with Jesus between them … Meanwhile standing near the cross of Jesus were his mother, and his mother's sister, Mary the wife of Clopas, and Mary Magdalene … So they put a sponge full of the wine on a branch of hyssop and held it to his mouth. When Jesus had received the wine, he said, "It is finished." Then he bowed his head and gave up his spirit … But when they came to Jesus and saw that he was already dead, they did not break his legs. Instead, one of the soldiers pierced his side with a spear, and at once blood and water came out.' [John 19.18 - 34]

THE CRUCIFIXION

Unfortunately we have lost the great majority of this picture. Buckler's sketch gave very little information, just a torso and part of Jesus' foot. Fortunately, as with other small details like the two-handed scourge mentioned above, the restoration of the north wall in 1987 revealed quite a bit more. The torso turns out to be a little man hammering the nail into Jesus' feet which are spurting more gouts of blood. Behind the hammerer are the shadowy remains of a figure, while on the other side of Jesus' feet are a pair of dark legs. On either side of Jesus we can see, suspended in mid-air, the feet of the two thieves being crucified with him.

The Passion scene from the Trinity College manuscript (Fig 59) gives us an idea of the probable composition of this scene. The little man is busy with hammer and nail at the bottom centre, the man on the right holds the bucket in one hand while proffering the sponge on the hyssop stick to Jesus' lips, and the man on the left behind the hammerer sticks the lance into Jesus' side. So once again we have three cameos in the one picture. What a pity we have lost most of it!

The picture from the Holkham Picture Bible, now in the British Library, Fig 60, shows the man with the sponge on the hyssop stick and the two thieves on either side of Jesus, with their feet at about the same positions as in our painting. Our painting probably combined the Holkham Bible's two crucified thieves with the scene in the Trinity College manuscript.

The Crucifixion is the fifth of the five Sorrowful Mysteries.

Fig 58. What remains of the Crucifixion scene

Fig 59. The Crucifixion scene from the Trinity College manuscript

Fig 60. The Crucifixion from the 14th C Holkham Picture Bible. British Library Board 09/06/2016, Add.47682, f.32

Fig 61.

'After these things, Joseph of Arimathea, who was a disciple of Jesus, though a secret one because of his fear of the Jews, asked Pilate to let him take away the body of Jesus. Pilate gave him permission; so he came and removed his body.' [John 19.38]

THE DESCENT FROM THE CROSS

This is one of the better preserved paintings on the north wall and gives us a good idea of what the previous picture must have looked like. In the centre, Christ hangs lifeless, his weight supported by Joseph of Arimathea (centre left) and Nicodemus (centre right standing) while a servant kneeling (centre right) removes the nail from Jesus' feet. On the left of the picture the grieving Mary tenderly kisses Jesus' tortured arm, in a pose reminiscent of many *pieta* paintings. On the right, now only faintly visible, stands Saint John whom Jesus 'made' Mary's son from the Cross (St. John chapter 19 verses 26 and 27). Jesus' wounds in hands, feet and side are obviously shown in the artist's characteristic way, but this picture is also an excellent example of the freedom of style and composition which our artist gave to all our paintings and also of the tender reverence in which he represents Mary throughout the whole scheme.

The Gough Psalter has a very similar composition of this scene (Fig 63). The same scene can also be seen in the Jonsberg altar piece, see page 89, and the Soissons Diptych on page 104.

Fig 62. The Descent from the Cross

Fig 63. The same scene from the Gough Psalter

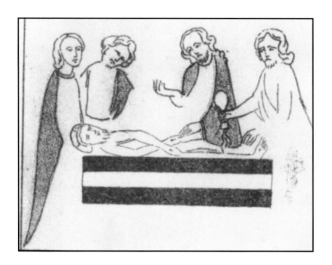

Fig 64.

'Nicodemus, who had first come to Jesus by night, also came, bringing a mixture of myrrh and aloes, weighing about a hundred pounds. They took the body of Jesus and wrapped it with the spices in linen cloths, according to the burial custom of the Jews. Now there was a garden in the place where he was crucified, and in the garden there was a new tomb in which no one had ever been laid. And so, because it was the Jewish day of Preparation, and the tomb was nearby, they laid Jesus there.' [John 19.39 - 42]

THE ANOINTING OF THE BODY

This scene was previously identified as 'The Entombment', but in medieval iconography that is a different picture and our painting is correctly identified by Stephen Maynard as 'The Anointing of the Body'.

All the characters from the previous scene are here. On the left Joseph of Arimethea cradles Jesus' head in his hands, while next to him Mary bows her head in mourning. No longer visible, Saint John kneels in front of Mary but behind the slab on which Jesus lies. Next to him Nicodemus holds a bottle of ointment in his right hand (the bottle has disappeared too) and holds Jesus' hand in his left hand. Behind him the servant pours oil from a bottle on to Jesus' body; we can see the bulb of the bottle but not the servant.

A lot of this scene is lost or indistinct and we have to rely on Buckler's sketch and a similar picture from the Gough Psalter (Fig 66) to get an idea of what it really was like.

Fig 65. The Anointing of the Body

Fig 66. The Gough Psalter's version of the picture gives us an idea of what has been lost from our wall painting

Fig 67.

'And the Lord stretched forth his hand and made the sign of the cross over Adam and over all his saints, and he took the right hand of Adam and went up out of hell, and all the saints followed him.' [Acts of Pilate p.139 The Apochryphal New Testament by M R James]

We now move to the bottom of the east wall on the left hand side for the next scene which is called

THE HARROWING OF HELL

Jesus stands on the left rather nonchalantly holding a staff (probably the vexillum but the cross piece and pennant are no longer visible) with his right hand and leading with his left hand Adam and Eve and the souls of the just from the jaws of hell, represented by a gaping serpent's jaws. Unfortunately, whilst Buckler's drawing clearly shows the serpent's jaws, they have by now disappeared from view, all except for one large fang which thrusts up between Adam's legs and a second fang behind the legs of the second standing person. The picture signifies Christ's victory over Satan and the powers of Hell, and the freeing of the pre-Incarnation just from their bonds. The picture from the Gough Psalter (Fig 70) is more elaborate but shows similar positioning of the figures. A similar, but later, picture from a painted reredos in Saint Maurice Cathedral in Angers, France, (Fig 69) has Jesus and the jaws of hell in the same positions as ours.

Note also the lines of inscription across the top of this scene. This is dealt with fully on page 95.

48

Fig 68. The Harrowing of Hell. Note the upturned fang of Hell's jaws in the centre between the legs of the central character

Fig 69. The 15th century painted reredos in Saint Maurice Cathedral in Angers, France, showing the Harrowing of Hell

Fig 70. The same scene from the Gough Psalter

Fig 71.

' ... an angel of the Lord, descending from heaven, came and rolled back the stone and sat on it ... For fear of him the guards shook and became like dead men. But the angel said to the women, "Do not be afraid; I know that you are looking for Jesus who was crucified. He is not here; for he has been raised, as he said ... ". Suddenly Jesus met them and said "Greetings!" And they came to him, took hold of his feet and worshipped him.'
(Matthew, chapter 28, verses 2 to 9)

THE RESURRECTION

This picture is immediately above the Harrowing of Hell. It shows Christ, once again wearing a cloak, rising from the tomb with the vexillum in his left hand, while he raises his right hand in blessing. Two angels escort him and three Roman soldiers sleep on undisturbed, underneath the arches. The signs of His crucifixion, the stigmata, are clearly visible in Christ's side, hands and feet. The tomb is shown as a typical medieval tomb such as can be seen locally in Dorchester Abbey, or Christ Church Cathedral in Oxford, and not as a rock tomb with a stone rolled away from its mouth which is how it is described in the New Testament.

The picture is a standard representation of this important scene which can be seen in many contemporary manuscripts, for example the Gough Psalter in the Bodleian Library. The French carved ivory diptych in the British Museum (Fig 73) has an almost identical picture but without the arches and Roman soldiers. See also the Soissons Diptych on page 105.

The Resurrection is the first of the five Glorious Mysteries.

Fig 72. The Resurrection. Note the Roman soldiers asleep underneath the arches

Fig 73. The Resurrection from the French ivory Diptych c.1350 AD. See also the Soissons Diptych on page 105.

Fig 74.

'Then he led them out as far as Bethany, and, lifting up his hands, he blessed them. While he was blessing them, he withdrew from them and was carried up into heaven.' [Luke 24.50]

THE ASCENSION

The final scene in the life of Christ is above the Resurrection scene and shows the Virgin Mary and the Apostles watching as Christ's feet and the bottom of his cloak disappear above them into the clouds.

Again this is a fairly 'standard' representation of this scene, but there are subtle differences compared with the picture from the Gough Psalter shown here. For example Mary's hands are clasped together in prayer in our picture, and the Apostles are more crowded than in the two rows shown in the Gough Psalter (Fig 76).

Note Saint Peter on the left with his keys and Saint John on the right next to Mary, holding a yellow chalice which is also his symbol.

The Ascension is the second of the five Glorious Mysteries.

As the wall paintings and stained glass windows would have formed a single scheme, it is possible that the east window of the church would have contained a representation of Christ in Glory, this being the culmination of the Life of Christ. See also page 80.

Fig 75. The Ascension as it is today

Fig 76. The Ascension from the Gough Psalter

Turning now to the south wall, what strikes us immediately is how much better preserved these paintings are. This is probably due to two reasons, firstly the sun does not fall on them causing the chemical reaction between salts in the moisture and the plaster creating crystals and hence erosion of the pigments, and secondly they were treated by Eve Baker using modern conservation techniques some ten years before the north wall was treated.

There are two 'stories' on the south wall, the General Resurrection or Last Judgement on the right hand side and the Death and Assumption of the Virgin Mary, which includes a third story about Saint Thomas and the Girdle.

THE DEATH AND ASSUMPTION OF MARY

As the early church developed after the Resurrection, there were not a few deviations and heresies, and inevitably besides the Gospels of Matthew, Mark, Luke and John there were other stories written down which purported to be about true happenings but which were, for the most part, fanciful inventions. These are known as the apocryphal gospels and have appeared in different forms throughout the ages, including some of the medieval Mystery Plays. The modern student can read them in M R James' excellent book *The Apocryphal New Testament*, but at the time of our wall paintings you would have had to read the Narrative of Joseph of Arimathea about the Assumption of the Blessed Virgin Mary or the Golden Legend by Jacobus de Varrazzo, also known as Jacobus de Voragine, the Archbishop of Genova from 1292 to 1298, who took a number of

the apocryphal writings and put them together in his book which was later printed by Caxton. The Golden Legend gives the stories of the Saints in the calendar sequence of their Saint's days throughout the year. You might also have heard and seen the story portrayed in a Mystery Play.

Our wall paintings of The Death and Assumption of Mary, whilst in generally better condition than the Life of Christ on the opposite wall, have suffered during their hidden years from having two massive marble memorials placed on top of them. I am often asked if there are likely to be the remains of the paintings behind the memorials but I fear that most of the plaster, and therefore paintings, will have been removed so that the memorials could be set into and held securely by the wall. However, where these memorials have destroyed the original paintings, we can make an educated guess as to what the original paintings portrayed.

Again the sequence of 'reading' on all three tiers is from the west towards the east window, except that for the moment we ignore the painting to the west of the westernmost south window, the General Resurrection (see pages 82 to 85).

EAST   WEST

| S14 Burial of The Virgin p.70 | S11 Conversion & Healing of Jews p.69 | S10 Conversion of chief priest p.68 | S9 Funeral of the Virgin p.66 | S1 General Resurrection or Last Judgement p.82 |

| S15 The Apostles at Table p. 74 | S13 John the Baptist p.90 | S12 John the Evangelist p.90 | S8 Death of the Virgin p.64 | S7 Virgin, Apostles, two widows, three widows & a donor p.62 | S2 St. Bartholomew p.92 |

| S16 ? p.76 | | | S6 ? p.60 | S5 The Virgin at Prayer p.58 | S4 Presentation of the Palm p.56 | S3 St. Laurence p.92 |

E5 Saint Paul p.80	E8 Coronation p.78
	E7 Assumption p.72
	E6 Thomas Receives the Girdle p.72

SOUTH

Fig 77. The arrangement of the wall paintings on the south wall and the south side of the east wall

55

Fig 78.

'One day the Virgin's heart was aflame with desire to be with her Son; she was so deeply stirred in spirit that her tears flowed abundantly. She could not with serenity of soul bear his being taken away for a time and the loss of his consoling presence. Then behold, an angel stood before her amid a great light and greeted her reverently as the mother of his Lord. "Hail, blessed Mary!" he said, "receive the blessing of him who bestowed salvation on Jacob. See, Lady, I have brought you a palm branch from paradise, and you are to have it carried before your bier. Three days from now you will be assumed from the body, because your Son is waiting for you, his venerable mother".' [The Golden Legend Vol.2, p.78]

THE PRESENTATION OF THE PALM

The story begins when the Angel (right) brings Mary the Palm of Paradise and announces that the hour approaches for her reunion with her Divine Son. Behind Mary to our left there are some black drapes, which are in fact Mary's blue gown which she has removed so that she can wear the pink coloured 'clothes of immortality' brought for her by the Angel.

In the carved ivory plaque by the Master of Kremsmunster on the Upper Rhine, dated to the last years of the 14th Century (Fig 173 on page 103), we see in the top left hand corner the presentation of the palm, Fig 80.

At Pamplona Cathedral in Spain there is a beautifully carved stone sequence of images of Mary's Death and Assumption above the doorway from the cloisters into the cathedral, known as La Puerta Preciosa. Fig 81 shows the Angel on the left handing the palm to Mary on the right. Note that Mary is wearing a headscarf.

See also the left hand side of the historiated letter M in Fig 84 on page 59.

In later representations of this scene, particularly in some Italian masterpieces, the Annunciation and the Presentation of the Palm become almost the same and are only distinguishable by seeing if it is a lily or a palm leaf which the Angel is giving to Mary.

Fig 79. The Presentation of the Palm of Paradise

Fig 80. Presentation of the Palm from the carved ivory diptych by the Master of Kremsmunster. See also page 103 for the complete diptych

Fig 81. The Angel handing the Palm to Mary from La Puerta Preciosa in Pamplona Cathedral, Spain. Sadly the stone palm branch has been broken off at some time

57

Fig 82.

*'Then Mary put off her garments and clothed herself in
her best raiment, and taking the palm which she had
received of the angel's hand she went out into the Mount
of Olivet and began to pray and to say: ... I pray thee,
O king of glory, that no power of hell may hurt me.
...'* [The Assumption:Latin narrative of Pseudo-
Melito from The Apochryphal New Testament by
M R James]

THE VIRGIN AT PRAYER

The second scene in the sequence then, shows
Mary kneeling in prayer, wearing the pink robe,
facing towards our left and with a blessing hand
floating in the air above her head. Here the Virgin
is praying to be preserved from the sight of the
Evil One at the moment of her death. The dark
blue robe she has removed hangs behind her - she
has replaced her mortal robes with the 'robes of
immortality'.

In the picture from the c.1310 manuscript Queen
Mary's Psalter, Fig 84, Mary is still wearing her
blue gown as she prays and God's head and arm
are shown coming out of the cloud to bless her.
Again we have a mirror image of the wall painting
with Mary facing to the right instead of to the left.

Fig 83. Mary praying - the scene as it is now

Fig 84. An historiated letter M shows Gabriel presenting the palm to Mary on the left and Mary praying on the right. This is from the Queen Mary Psalter, c.1310. British Library Board 09/06/2016, Royal MS 2 B VII f.296v

Fig 85.

'As Mary was praying and saying Amen, behold, suddenly the apostle John arrived on a cloud. And he knocked on Mary's door, opened it, and went in … and she showed him her funeral garments … saying, "Father John, you know everything that I have in this big house except my funeral garments and two tunics. There are two widows here: when I go forth from the body, give one to each". After she said these things, she brought him to where the palm staff was, which had been given to her by the angel, so that the apostles would take it. And she said to him, "Father John, take this palm staff, so that you may carry it before me, for this is why it was given to me".' [Ancient traditions of the Virgin Mary's dormition and assumption, Appendix B The earliest Greek Dormition Narrative, pp.358 - 360]

DAMAGED SCENE – THE VIRGIN, SAINT JOHN AND TWO WIDOWS

The third picture is mostly obscured by the memorial to the Rev'd Francis Markham, who was Vicar at the time of the Restoration of the Monarchy and who died shortly afterwards in 1668. All that remains of the painting shows two ladies on the left, both wearing a medieval headdress, one a barbette and fillet and the other a wimple, and part of a figure on the right facing towards them.

In the sequence of the story from the Golden Legend, Mary presents the Palm from Paradise to Saint John the Evangelist, and in fact right next to this painting, in the window splay, we see Saint John holding the Palm (see page 90). So it seems quite likely that this painting originally showed the two widows, wearing medieval headdresses, who we can just make out on the left, with Mary in front of them handing the Palm to John on the right. A reconstruction of this scene is shown in Fig 87. We shall see the two widows again in the next scene.

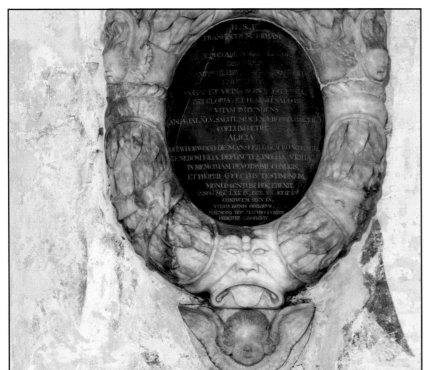

Fig 86. The scene covered by the Markham Memorial

Fig 87. A reconstruction of how this scene may have looked originally

61

Fig 88.

'When she had said these things, Mary called Peter and all the apostles…after this she went out and sat down in their midst…And after praying she went in and lay down on her bed, and she fulfilled the course of her life…And at about the third hour, there was a great thunder and a sweet smelling fragrance, so that everyone was driven off to sleep by the exceedingly sweet smell, except for only the three virgins. He caused them to remain awake so that they could testify concerning the funeral of Mary the mother of our Lord and her glory.'
[Ancient traditions of the Virgin Mary's dormition and assumption, Appendix B The earliest Greek Dormition Narrative, pp.363 - 364]

THE VIRGIN'S FAREWELL TO THE APOSTLES, THREE VIRGINS, TWO WIDOWS AND A DONOR

The next picture in the sequence is immediately above the presentation of the palm, in the centre tier, and shows Mary in the centre with the apostles to the left facing her and six female 'neighbours' behind her. The story tells us that the apostles were all miraculously transported to where Mary was – we see them all seated except for one, probably Saint John, who stands behind the foremost apostle who is probably Saint Peter (as he is tonsured). Behind Mary we see six female figures, three standing at the back and three kneeling in front of them. All have their hands clasped in prayer. In the back row on the right we recognise the two widows from the previous scene, one wearing barbette and fillet and the other a wimple. Then there are three young women with no headdresses, who are therefore the three virgins in the story. This leaves the richly dressed woman in a headdress kneeling in the front row immediately next to Mary. Her sleeves are the height of fashion for the time and it seems most likely that she is Lady Barentin, representing the donors of the paintings.

I have found two similar pictures to match the two sides of our painting, the Apostles on the left hand side being similar to those in the series of paintings called the Maesta by the Italian painter Duccio di Buoninsegna (c.1260 - 1318), (Fig 90), which are now in the Municipal Museum in Siena. The six women on the right are similar to the five women and one King in the scene from the manuscript Hungarian Anjou Legendary, Fig 91, now in the Vatican Library.

Fig 89. Mary in the centre, the Apostles on the left and the three virgins, two widows and Lady Barentin on the right

Fig 90. Mary takes leave of the Apostles from Duccio's Maesta, now in the Municipal Museum in Siena. © 2016. Photo Opera Metropolitana Siena/SCALA, Florence.

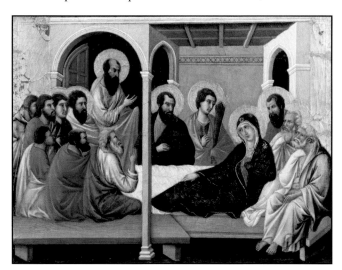

Fig 91 right. Mary with three virgins, two other women and a donor King, (possibly Charles I of Hungary) from the Hungarian Anjou Legendary made in Bologna in 1330 and now in the Vatican Library.   Vat.lat.8541 0009 fa 0001r © 2016 Biblioteca Apostolica Vaticana.

Fig 92.

'About the third hour of the night Jesus came with companies of angels, troops of prophets, hosts of martyrs, a legion of confessors and choirs of virgins, and all took their places before the Virgin's throne and sang dulcet canticles ... Then Mary's soul went forth from her body and flew to the arms of her Son ...' [The Golden Legend Vol.2, p79 - 80]

THE DEATH OF THE VIRGIN

To the left of the previous picture we see the death of Mary. Again this picture is partly damaged by the Markham memorial but we have enough of it to be able to see what is going on. The angels are clearly visible on the left and Jesus in the centre but we have lost most of Mary's body because of the memorial. The apostles are on the right, standing but asleep according to the story! and Mary lies on her deathbed across the centre, while behind her body we see her soul escorted by two angels rising to heaven. Again this scene is represented in the bottom row of the carved ivory plaque by the Master of Kremsmünster (Fig 95) in mirror image, and we also see it in the Italian manuscript (Fig 94) where Mary's soul is shown like a small baby wrapped in swaddling bands.

Fig 93. The Death of the Virgin Mary, partly obscured by the top of the Markham memorial

Fig 94. The scene from an Italian manuscript

Fig 95. The Master of Kremsmunster's representation of the scene. See also page 103 for the complete diptych

Fig 96.

'Then the apostles reverently lifted the body and placed it on a bier. ... Peter and Paul then lifted the bier and Peter began to sing ... the other apostles took up the chant ... Angels were present too, singing with the apostles ... The populace was excited ... and came rushing out of the city to see what was going on. Then someone said: "The disciples of Jesus are carrying Mary away dead, and singing around her the melody you hear." At once they hurried to take arms and exhorted each other saying: "Come on, let us kill all those disciples and burn the body that bore the seducer." The chief priest ... said: "Look at the tabernacle of that man who disturbed us and our people so much! Look at the glory that is now paid to that woman!" After saying this he put his hands on the litter, intending to overturn it and throw the corpse to the ground. But suddenly his hands withered and stuck to the bier, so that he was hanging by his hands; and he moaned and cried in great pain, while the rest of the people were stricken with blindness by angels.'
[The Golden Legend Vol.2, p.81]

THE FUNERAL OF THE VIRGIN

This scene is above the neighbours and apostles scene, and shows the funeral procession. At the front is Saint John the Evangelist carrying the Palm, leading two groups of apostles who carry Mary's coffin by means of two poles on their shoulders. The coffin is draped with an elaborately patterned cloth and is surmounted at each end with a cross. Note the marching feet of the apostles.

In the centre of the scene we see three small figures all suffering from their contact with the bier.

Our picture is a fairly standard representation of this scene, and part of a similar version can be seen in the church at Croughton in Northamptonshire.

The funeral procession takes centre stage on the west end of the cathedral in Amiens, France, Fig 98. A similar scene can be seen on the embroidered Syon cope in the Victoria and Albert Museum (Fig 99).

Fig 97. The Funeral Procession of the Virgin

Fig 98. The funeral procession on the west end of Amiens cathedral in France

Fig 99. The same scene from the Syon Cope – see page 102

67

Fig 100.

'The chief priest cried out: "Holy Peter, do not scorn me in this extremity! Pray the Lord for me, I beg of you! You must remember how I stood by you and defended you when the portress accused you." Peter answered: "... if you believe in our Lord Jesus Christ and in this woman who conceived and bore him, I hope you will quickly receive the benefit of health." The chief priest said: "I believe that the Lord Jesus is the true Son of God, and that this woman was his most holy mother." At once his hands were loosed from the bier, but his arms were still withered and the pain was as severe as before. Peter told him: "Kiss the bier and say, 'I believe in Jesus Christ God, whom this woman carried in her womb and remained a virgin after she delivered her child.'" He did as he was told and was cured instantly.' [The Golden Legend Vol.2, p81]

CONVERSION OF THE CHIEF PRIEST·

This is the small two-character picture to the left of the previous one. The chief priest kneels in front of Saint John the Evangelist who holds the Palm of Paradise in one hand while with the other he sprinkles holy water over the chief priest using an aspergillum (wand).

I have been unable to find any other representations of this scene or the next, the Conversion and Healing of the Blinded Jews, page 69. Fortunately these two scenes are in fairly good condition, which is a good thing if, indeed, they are as rare as they appear to be.

Fig 101. Saint John the Evangelist converts the
· chief priest

Fig 102.

'Peter then told him: "Take the palm from the hand of our brother John and hold it up over the people who have been blinded. Those who are willing to believe will receive their sight, those who refuse will never see again."' [The Golden Legend Vol.2, p.81]

CONVERSION AND HEALING OF THE BLINDED JEWS

This is a unique picture in that it does not appear in any of the authoritative catalogues of medieval iconography, nor have I so far found any similar pictures in embroidery, manuscripts or other media. The chief priest, wearing a flat hat and sporting a beard, stands with the Palm of Paradise in his hand addressing his followers. In the words of a medieval mystery play, 'Ye Jews that langour in this great infirmity, believeth in Christ Jesu and ye shall have health, through virtue of this holy palm that comes from the trinity, your sickness shall assuage and restore you to wealth'.

So they were all converted and restored to health.

Fig 103. The Conversion and Healing of the Blinded Jews

Fig 104.

'The apostles now took Mary's body and laid it in the tomb.   Then as the Lord had commanded, they sat around the sepulchre.' [The Golden Legend Vol.2., p.81]

THE BURIAL OF THE VIRGIN

We now move to the left of the left-hand window still in the top tier. Mary's body is laid in a red sarcophagus by a woman on the right and Saint John to the left of her (now mostly disappeared). There were probably other figures in this scene — Buckler's sketch shows four definitely, with the extra two at the left hand end of the tomb.

The scene from the manuscript picture in Queen Mary's Psalter from the British Library (Fig 106) shows a larger number of people around Mary's body.

Fig 105. Mary's body is laid in the tomb

Fig 106. The same scene from Queen Mary's Psalter. British Library Board 09/06/2016, Royal MS 2.B. VII, f.298a

'Thomas was suddenly brought to the Mount of Olives and saw the holy body being taken up, and cried out to Mary: "Make thy servant glad by thy mercy, for now thou goest to heaven". And the girdle with which the apostles had girt the body was thrown down to him; he took it and went to the valley of Josaphat.' [The Apocryphal New Testament, p.217]

Fig 107.

The careful arrangement of the pictures in narrative sequence is upset because of the artist's desire to have the crowning of Mary as Queen of Heaven on the east wall opposite the picture of Christ's Ascension. After this picture of the Assumption, we return on pages 74 and 75 to the east wall and the centre and bottom pictures on the south side.

The Assumption is the third of the five Glorious Mysteries.

THE ASSUMPTION and

SAINT THOMAS RECEIVES THE GIRDLE

The apochryphal Joseph of Arimethea narrative tells how, three days after her death, the angels bring Mary's soul back to her body and carry her up to heaven. The story is believed to have originated in Syria in the sixth century AD.

At this point St. Thomas, who was saying Mass in India, is suddenly transported to the Mount of Olives where he witnesses Mary's body being carried up to heaven by a host of angels. He cries out to Mary in joy and her girdle is dropped down to him. Our pictures show Thomas at the left hand side of the empty tomb, with the girdle in his hand, while above the empty tomb, the Virgin floats upwards with her hands at prayer, supported by two angels. Only one of them remains very visible on the left with head, shoulders and wings and one hand grasping Mary's elbow.

Visible across Thomas' head and stretching to the right is the second inscription described in more detail on page 95.

The accompanying painting on wood in Llandaff Cathedral (Fig 110) shows the Virgin surrounded by a host of angels with the girdle in her hand, while Thomas kneels at the bottom centre. Whereas in the stained glass window at The Assumption of the Blessed Virgin Mary Church at Beckley, just north of Oxford, angels are seen carrying Mary up in what looks like a blanket but was probably meant to represent her shroud. (Fig 109).

Fig 108. The Assumption and Thomas receiving the Girdle, as it is today

Fig 109. The scene in the east window of the Church of the Assumption of the Blessed Virgin Mary at Beckley, Oxfordshire

Fig 110. The scene on a painted wooden panel in Llandaff Cathedral, with a tiny figure of Thomas at the bottom centre

Fig 111.

'When he (Thomas) had greeted the apostles, Peter said: "Thou wast always unbelieving, and so the Lord hath not suffered thee to be at his mother's burial." ... Then he said: "Where have ye laid her body?" and they pointed to the sepulchre. But he said: "The holy body is not there." Peter said: "Formerly you would not believe in the resurrection of the Lord before you touched him; how should you believe us?" Thomas went on saying: "It is not here." Then in anger they went and took away the stone, and the body was not there; and they knew not what to say, being vanquished by Thomas' words. Then Thomas told them how he had been saying mass in India (and he still had on his priestly vestments), how he had been brought to the Mount of Olives and seen the ascension of Mary and she had given him her girdle: and he showed it. They all rejoiced and asked his pardon, and he blessed them and said: Behold how good and pleasant a thing it is, brethren, to dwell together in unity.' [The Apochryphal New Testament pp. 217, 218]

THE APOSTLES AT TABLE

This scene is in the centre of the wall below the Burial of the Virgin and shows five apostles gathered round a table with a sixth figure facing them at the left-hand (east) end. There is bread on the table, a jug and a cup. Being adjacent to the high altar of the church, has the artist painted the apostles celebrating the eucharist? If so then Saint Thomas, left, is interrupting them to show them the girdle.

I have not yet found another representation of this exact scene. Sadly our painting has been badly affected by damp and we have lost some of the detail, but we are fortunate that Professor Tristram made a detailed drawing of the scene in 1933, Fig 114 , which helps us to interpret what remains.

The Virgin's Girdle, *La Sacra Cintola*, is the holy relic of the Cathedral of Santo Stefano of Prato in Italy and is shown to the people five times a year, and especially on the Feast of the Assumption. In the stained glass window at Beckley (Fig 109) the Girdle is coloured green and the relic in Prato is made of fine green wool with gold tassels, Fig 112 below.

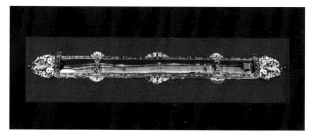

Fig 112. The Sacra Cintola in Santo Stefano Cathedral, Prato, Italy

Fig 113. Thomas shows the girdle to the Apostles

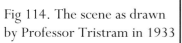

Fig 114. The scene as drawn by Professor Tristram in 1933

THE APOSTLES AT THE EMPTY TOMB (?)

The next picture in the sequence is then the one below the previous one, and now obliterated by the memorial to Katherine Villiers, the daughter of the Rev'd George Villiers, one-time Vicar of Chalgrove.

It is possible that this showed the apostles standing at the empty tomb having gone there in disbelief at Thomas' claim that Mary's body was not there. One account of the story states that the empty tomb was filled with flowers. All that we can see, however, is a small head to the top and left of the Villiers memorial, Fig 116.

Was this picture perhaps like the bottom half of the painting of the Assumption by Bartolomeo della Gatta (Fig 117), which is now in the Diocesan Museum in Cortona, in which the apostles stand around the flower filled tomb?

Fig 115. The Villiers memorial

Fig 116. The head top left of the Villiers memorial

Fig 117. The Assumption and Thomas receiving the Girdle, by Bartolomeo della Gatta, 15thC, now in the Diocesan Museum in Cortona, Italy

Fig 118.

THE CORONATION OF THE VIRGIN

The final picture in the sequence is above The Assumption and shows Mary on the left sitting on a bench next to and facing Jesus on the right who raises his hand over her head, either in blessing or, more likely, to place a crown upon her head. Above their heads there are what remains of two angels.

This is again a fairly popular and standard representation of this scene which can be seen in many manuscripts, as well as ivories such as the French 14th century ivory on display in the Victoria & Albert Museum, and again in the east window at Beckley Church (Fig 120) just outside Oxford. There is also a good mosaic picture of this scene by Gaddo Gaddi on the west end wall of the Duomo in Florence dating from the 1340s.

The Coronation of the Virgin is the fourth of the five Glorious Mysteries.

'… on this day the celestial militia came to meet the mother of God with festive celebration and shone round about her with dazzling light, leading her up to the throne of God with lauds and spiritual canticles, and that the army of the heavenly Jerusalem exulted with indescribable joy, and welcomed her with ineffable devotion and boundless rejoicing….the Saviour himself went to meet his mother joyfully and gladly placed her on a throne at his side.' [The Golden Legend Vol 2. page 84]

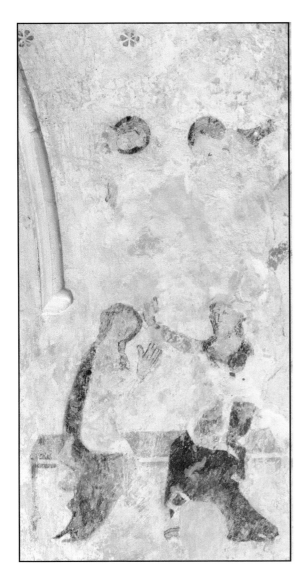

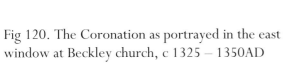

Fig 120. The Coronation as portrayed in the east window at Beckley church, c 1325 – 1350AD

Fig 119. Mary is crowned as Queen of Heaven. Mary and Jesus sit on a bench and Jesus on the right places the crown on Mary's head, while angels fly down from above

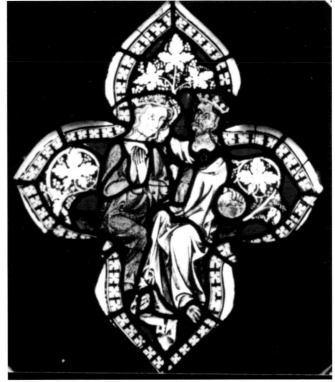

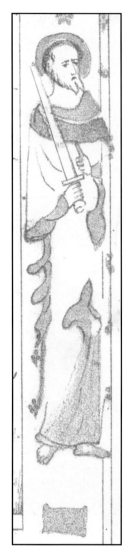

Fig 121. Saint Peter and Saint Paul

'So (Nero) the emperor gave Peter and Paul into the hands of Paulinus … Then Peter, being an alien, was condemned to be crucified, while Paul, because he was a Roman citizen, was sentenced to beheading.' [The Golden Legend, Vol 1. pp 344, 345]

SAINT PETER

To the left of the east window is a large representation of Saint Peter, who holds in his left hand the keys to the Kingdom of Heaven and in his right hand a book (which is no longer visible). The artist has painted the keys so that they also look like an inverted cross. In 'The Golden Legend' we are told that 'when Peter came to the cross he said "Because my Lord came down from heaven to earth, his cross was raised straight up; but he deigns to call me from earth to heaven, and my cross should have my head toward the earth and should point my feet toward heaven. Therefore, since I am not worthy to be on the cross the way my Lord was, turn my cross and crucify me head down!" So they turned the cross and nailed him to it with his feet upwards and his hands downwards.'

SAINT PAUL

Opposite him on the right hand side of the east window is Saint Paul, with his emblem, a sword, nonchalantly resting on his shoulder. Paul was martyred by being beheaded with a sword, a right he claimed as a Roman citizen.

PETER, PAUL AND JESUS

More often than not when we find Peter and Paul in these relative positions, we find Jesus between them. Two examples of this are shown in Figs 124 and 125, from the Duomo in Taormina, Sicily, and the parish church in Checkendon. They are also clearly visible with their emblems on the Syon cope in the Victoria & Albert Museum (page 105), on either side of the crucifixion, and on the Brass memorial from the French Bishop's tomb, Fig 143 on page 91. For this reason I am fairly confident that our east window's medieval glass would have contained a representation of Christ.

Fig 122. Saint Peter on the left hand side of the east window

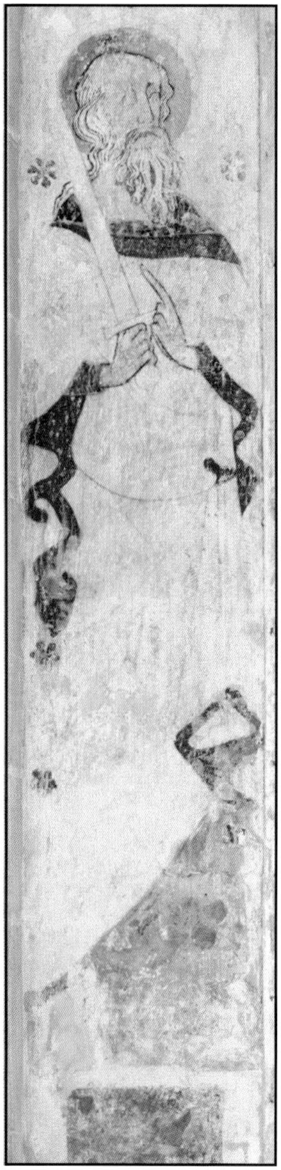

Fig 123. Saint Paul on the right hand side of the east window

Fig 124. Saint Peter and Saint Paul on either side of Jesus from a painted wooden altar piece in the Duomo of Taormina, Sicily, c.1320

Fig 125. The two Saints on either side of Jesus (above) on the east wall of SS Peter and Paul church in Checkendon, Oxfordshire

Fig 126.

THE GENERAL RESURRECTION OR LAST JUDGEMENT

In the south west corner of the chancel is a scene representing the Last Judgement. This is not strictly speaking a 'Doom' because it does not show the weighing of souls, nor the good going off to heaven while the bad are led away to hell. Such a Doom can be seen in the church of Saint James the Great at South Leigh just outside Witney in Oxfordshire.

Our General Resurrection, however, is incorporated into the main scheme of paintings in the chancel, because of Mary's association with the Last Judgement as a mediator for mankind. The scene is placed in the south west corner so that it can be viewed through the squint window from the side chapel.

At the top of the scene, Fig 127, Jesus clearly showing the stigmata in his hands, side and feet, sits on a rainbow signifying the covenant made by God with mankind after the Flood. Between his feet rests the disc of the world. Next to him, Mary kneels in supplication baring her breast, the meaning of this icon being that as she tenderly served Jesus as a baby so now must Jesus be tender, loving and merciful to humankind. To the left of Mary, an angel with a horn (sadly no longer visible) flies down the side of the window arch sounding the last trump, and behind her stands another angel holding a staff. To the right of Jesus there was also standing another angel but only an indication of his feet remain. Below them are two tiers of souls rising from their graves. The upper tier includes a Pope with the three chevrons on his hat, a Bishop wearing a mitre, and a Cardinal wearing a scarlet biretta (hat). In the lower tier there are two tonsured monks, ladies and men, some with crosses on their shrouds. On the right between the two tiers of souls and Jesus above are what is left of another angel flying down the side of the wall.

Overleaf Figs 128 and 129 show a comparison of the top of our painting with the similar scene from Queen Mary's Psalter, now in the British Library, and Fig 130 shows a similar wall painting of the General Resurrection in St. Mary's Church, Bazylika Mariacka, in Gdansk, Poland.

Fig 127. The General Resurrection

Fig 128. The top part of our General Resurrection painting

Fig 129. A similar picture from the Queen Mary's Psalter. British Library Board 09/06/2016, Royal MS 2.B.VII, f.302v

Fig 130. A General Resurrection wall painting in
the Bazylika Mariacka in Gdansk, Poland

Fig 131. Saint Helen, left, and Mary Magdalene, right, in the north east window of the Chancel.

SAINTS IN WINDOW ALCOVES

In all the chancel windows, except the window of The Annunciation, there are two saints, one on each side, and as in the main scheme of paintings they are drawn in such a way as to tell us who they are.

SAINT HELEN

In the north east window, on the left hand side is Saint Helen of the True Cross. The recent conservation of the paintings has revealed the position of the Cross and Helen's crown, and her right hand holding a book. Saint Helen is the patron saint of our sister church in this parish at Berrick Salome but her association with Mary is unclear. According to 'The Golden Legend', Volume 1, Chapter 68, Saint Helen was sent to Jerusalem by her son, Emperor Constantine (the Younger) to find the True Cross some 270 years after the Crucifixion. With aid of a Jewish wise man called Judas, Saint Helen found all three crosses and Jesus' cross was identified by the miracles it brought about. Today there are not many remaining images of Saint Helen and the one shown is a portion of stained glass window of the Norfolk School dating from the second half of the 15th century which can be seen in the V & A Museum (Fig 133).

Cleaning of this painting during the 2015/6 Conservation work revealed the outline of Saint Helen's crown and the position of the cross, Fig 134.

Fig 132. All that remains of Saint Helen of the True Cross today.

Fig 133. Saint Helen in a stained glass window of the Norwich School, second half of 15th century.

Fig 134. Drawing in the positions of Saint Helen's crown and cross from the remaining faint outlines

87

Fig 135. Mary Magdalene

SAINT MARY MAGDALENE

Opposite Saint Helen is what remains of Saint Mary Magdalene, (Fig 135), placed close to the Crucifixion scenes. Her right hand is held in a strange way and, although it has now disappeared, she probably held her emblem of the alabaster jar of spikenard oil with which she anointed Jesus' feet at the house in Bethany [John 12.3]. Her left hand is held up apparently indicating the crucifixion scene on the adjacent wall. She can be seen with her jar emblem in many paintings and statues, for example in the painting (Fig 137) on the underside of the sarcophagus of the Duchess of Suffolk in St. Mary's Church, Ewelme, Oxfordshire, although you have to prostrate yourself to be able to see it! She also has the jar tucked in her left arm in the painted miniature on the side of the golden head of the medieval Reichenau crozier, dated 1351AD, in the Victoria & Albert Museum (Figs 138 and 139).

But on the exquisitely carved wooden altar piece from Jonsberg in Sweden, (Fig 136) dating from the 1510s and now in the Historiska Museum in Stockholm, we find Mary Magdalene in a very similar pose to that depicted in our wall painting (only in mirror image). The scene of the Descent from the Cross, on the Jonsberg altar piece (Fig 140) shows Mary Magdalene in close proximity, as she is in our paintings.

Fig.136. Mary Magdalene in the Jonsberg Altarpiece

Fig 137. A copy of the painting of Mary Magdalene on the underside of the tomb of the Duchess of Suffolk in St. Mary's Church, Ewelme

Fig 139. A close up of Mary Magdalene on the Reichenau Crozier. © Victoria and Albert Museum, London

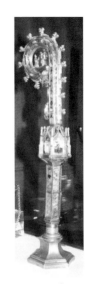

Fig 138. The Reichenau Crozier

Fig 140. The Descent from the Cross on the Jonsberg altar piece with Mary Magdalene in close attendance

Fig 141.

'In those days John the Baptist appeared in the wilderness of Judea ... Now John wore clothing of camel's hair with a leather belt around his waist, and his food was locusts and wild honey.' [Matthew 3 vv 1-4]

'The revelation of Jesus Christ, which God gave him to show his servants what must soon take place; he made it known by sending his angel to his servant John, who testified to the word of God and to the testimony of Jesus Christ, even to all that he saw.' [The Revelation 1 vv1 -2]

SAINT JOHN THE BAPTIST

Moving to the south east window, we find on the left hand side a man dressed in clothes of camel's hair and cradling in his left arm a halo ring containing a small lamb, the *Agnus Dei*, the Lamb of God. This is, of course, John the Baptist. Another ivory, the left side of a diptych, in the British Museum shows John in this posture (Fig 145). See also Fig 175 on page 105 for the whole of this side of the diptych.

SAINT JOHN THE EVANGELIST

Opposite him stands a young man holding the palm of paradise, which the Virgin Mary had given him. This is Saint John the Evangelist, placed close to the story of the death and assumption of Mary, in which he played an important part as we have read above. A brass memorial to an unknown 14th century Flemish Bishop, also in the British Museum, has a similar picture of John at the left hand side next to Saint Peter (Fig 143).

Fig 142. Saint John the Evangelist.

Fig 143. The brass from an unknown French Bishop's tomb showing Saint John the Evangelist (left) with the Palm of Paradise. © The Trustees of the British Museum. All rights reserved.

Fig 144. Saint John the Baptist in the wall paintings

Fig 145. Saint John the Baptist in a carved ivory diptych . See also page 105. © The Trustees of the British Museum. All rights reserved.

Fig 146. Saint Laurence left and Saint Bartholomew right in the south west window of the Chancel.

'(The Emperor) Decius said to Laurence: "Either you will sacrifice to the gods, or you will spend the night being tortured." Laurence: "My night has no darkness, and all things gleam in the light!" Decius gave his orders: "Let an iron bed be brought, and let this stubborn Laurence rest on it!". The executioners therefore stripped him, laid him out on the iron grill, piled burning coals under it, and pressed heated iron pitchforks upon his body.' [The Golden Legend, Vol II, p66]

'When Bartholomew was brought before him, the king said "So you are the one who subverted my brother!". The apostle: "I did not subvert him, I converted him!" … Hearing this, the king tore the purple robe he was wearing, and ordered the apostle to be beaten with clubs and flayed alive.' [The Golden Legend, Vol II, p112]

SAINT LAURENCE

Finally, in the south west window, on the left is Saint Laurence who was a Roman Deacon, hence the book which he holds in his right hand. He was martyred a few days after Pope Sixtus II in the persecution of the Emperor Valerian in 258AD. Legend has it that he was roasted alive on a gridiron, and with his left hand he points down to the gridiron standing in front of him. Another picture of Saint Laurence comes from Saint Cuthbert's stole, 934AD, which can be seen in the museum at Durham Cathedral (Fig 149).

SAINT BARTHOLEMEW

Opposite Saint Laurence stands Saint Bartholomew who holds in his hand a large flaying knife, by which, according to the Roman Martyrology, he was skinned alive before being beheaded at his martyrdom in Armenia. Saint Bartholomew is also to be seen on the Syon Cope in the Victoria & Albert Museum (page 105) and in the wooden retable from Ganthem Church, Sweden, c 1350AD, which can be seen in the Historiska Museum in Stockholm (Fig 150). He is the patron saint of tanners and also of lepers (those with skin diseases) and our painting is visible through the smaller squint in the opposite wall which was originally outside the east end of the north aisle when the chancel was painted.

Fig 147. Saint Laurence with his book and gridiron

Fig 148. Saint Bartholomew with his flaying knife

Fig 149. Saint Laurence on the embroidered stole of Saint Cuthbert in Durham Cathedral Museum

Fig 150. Saint Bartholomew on the wooden retable from Ganthem Church, Sweden

THE PAINTED CHURCH

As Clive Rouse points out in his book *Medieval Wall Paintings* "… all medieval churches in England were more or less completely painted".

The Conservation and Refurbishment project during 2015 and 2016 revealed other fragments of paintings on the walls of St. Mary's church so that we now know of paintings from seven different periods. Apart from the chancel scheme, these are as follows.

SAINT'S TABERNACLE

In the Saint James' chapel at the east end of the north aisle beside the window there is a painting of a tabernacle, or canopy, for the image of a saint, probably Saint James, Fig 151. There is a tower with three pinnacles from which fly banners. Underneath there are carved roof beams, and then below them the outline of an ogee shaped arch. The saint is no longer visible, if he were in fact painted on the wall. It is more likely that the saint would have been present as a carved and painted image in front of the wall painting. There are the remains of some indecipherable text towards the bottom of the painting.

In his will of 1452 Sir Drew Barentin III left the contents of the chapel at his manor to the newly created chapel, here, on the north side of the church, so we know that this painting dates to this time.

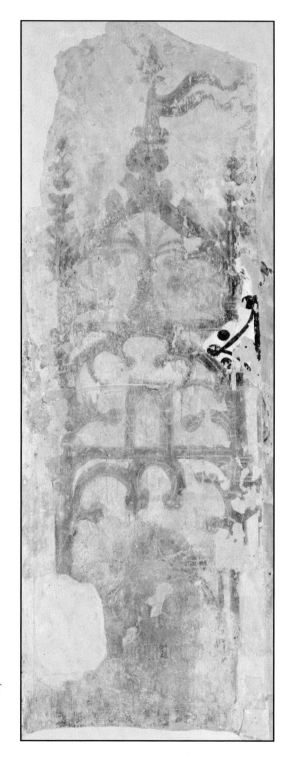

Fig 151. The original wall paintings on the east wall of the Saint James' Chapel. Note the over-painted motif on the right hand side - see pages 95 and 96

On the right hand side of the painting, adjacent to the window splay and just below the pinnacles at the top, there is a small amount of over-painting where some white limewash has been painted over the scene and a red motif then painted on top. See below for more information about this.

TEXTS IN THE CHANCEL

At the bottom of the Jesse Tree on the north wall, and across the Harrowing of Hell and Saint Thomas receiving the Girdle on the east wall of the chancel, there are several lines of text. They are difficult to read but it can be seen that they are in Latin. The one over the Jesse Tree is possibly the beginning of the *Pater Noster*, the Lord's Prayer, while the one over the Harrowing of Hell appears to be part of the Asperges, a prayer used in the Latin Mass which is taken from verse 7 of Psalm 51, '(Invoc)ate d(omi)n(u)m: Lavabis me a sup(er) nive(m) dealbabor', translated as 'Call on the Lord: "Wash me and I shall be made whiter than snow",' Fig 152. The text over Saint Thomas has not been deciphered but begins with the letter M with a cross on the top, which indicates that the word 'Maria' was written there, so it was probably a prayer to the Virgin Mary.

All three of these texts have been written over the

Fig 152. A close up of the lower part of the painting of the Harrowing of Hell showing the inscription.

original paintings at a later date. It is possible that they date to the period of Queen Mary's reign, 1553 to 1558, when the 'Counter Reformation' took place and the Queen encouraged the re-instatement of catholic practices that had been banned by Henry VIII and his son Edward VI. When Queen Elizabeth came to the throne in 1558 the use of Latin in the church's services was permanently banned.

BORDER MOTIF AND FLEUR DE LYS

The red motif over the edge of the saint's

Fig 153. Motif fragment over south porch doorway

tabernacle, mentioned above, has now been found in several other places. There were fragments of it in three places around the archway of the door from the south porch into the church, one of which has been preserved, Fig 153, and from which the artist's impression in Fig 154 has been made. The same motif was then discovered over the archway of the door from the north aisle to the outside, with a fleur

Fig 154. Artist's impression

de lys design at the apex of the arch, Fig 155. There were also fragments of the motif on the right hand edge of the window to the left of the north door and at the top of the arch of the

Fig 155. The fleur de lys and motif decoration over the north door

western window of the north aisle. So it is probable that this motif decorated all of the window and doorway arches of the nave. The motif in the south porch was painted onto a type of plaster which dates to earlier than 1600, and because the motif over the tabernacle was on an over-painting it seems likely that it was done after the reformation injunction of Edward VI in 1547. The presence of the fleur de lys in the decoration over the north door may be a reference to the Virgin Mary, so again this may date to the time of the Counter Reformation, or slightly later.

ZIG ZAG BORDER DECORATION

A later decorative border has been found in three places. Unusually two of these places are on the east and west walls of the south porch, Figs 156 and 157. These are on plaster made using horse hair, a technique which dates from early 1600, and appear to be borders of textual plaques. This is

Fig 156. Zig-zag decoration on east wall of the south porch

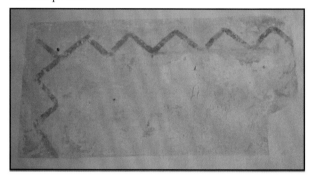

Fig 157. Zig-zag decoration on west wall of the porch

confirmed by the third location of this border on the north wall between the two windows to the east of the north door, Fig 158. Only three fragments of this large inscription remain, as the plaster had been replaced in places in past years, but enough remains to show us the complexity of the border with the red zig zag decorated with a green background and semi circular patterns. The text appears to be in English which confirms a post Reformation date.

PURITAN MOURNING DECORATION

While the work of the refurbishment project was being carried out, the memorials on the walls of the church were encased in wooden boxes to

Fig 158. Detail of one of the fragments of the text on the north wall of the church showing the vertical zig-zag border decoration

Fig 159. The mourning decoration at the top of the Winchcombe memorial

1984 and was then placed in its present position. When it was removed the tabernacle mentioned above (page 94) was revealed.

protect them from damage. Just above the box protecting the Winchcombe memorial in the north aisle, the remains of a painted 'ball' was found. Later during the project, after the protective box had been removed, this ball was shown to be part of a puritan mourning device, Fig 159, which probably preceded the erection of the marble memorial to Christian Winchcombe, who died in 1557. The monument was erected after the death of her son Benedict who died in 1623 and also records her husband Thomas, her father Henrie Bradshawe, Lord Chiefe Barron of the Exchequer, and her son-in-law William Hall. This fragmentary painted decoration has been limewashed over for preservation.

THE QUATREMAINE MEMORIAL

At the west end of the Nave on the wall adjacent to the bell tower is a painted memorial to members of the Quatremaine family dating from 1692, Fig 160. Such painted memorials are rare in England. This memorial used to be on the east wall of the Saint James' Chapel on the north side of the window but was carefully removed for cleaning and restoration by the late Eve Baker in

Fig 160. The Quatremaine Memorial on the west wall of the Nave

THE CONSERVATION AND REFURBISHMENT PROJECT 2015 TO 2016

From 1st June 2015 to 3rd April 2016 the church was closed for a £1.2 million programme of conservation and refurbishment which was funded partly by the Heritage Lottery Fund and other grant aiding bodies, and by local fund raising.

The chancel and the nave were filled with scaffolding, providing work platforms at three levels. In the chancel, Fig 161, this enabled the conservation of the complete scheme of medieval wall paintings described in this guide, as well as the cleaning and conservation of the ceiling, the installation of the new lighting scheme and sound system, the refurbishment of the Barentin brass memorials, the replacement of damaged stone tiles in the floor and the re-plastering of the lower walls.

Fig 161. Cleaning and conserving the medieval wall paintings in the chancel

Fig 162. Cleaning the roof timbers in the nave

In the nave, Fig 162, the ceiling was cleaned and redecorated, the walls re-plastered and decorated, new lighting and heating installed, a sound loop and complete sound system installed and damage to the floor tiling repaired or replaced.

During the first few weeks, our wall paintings conservator, Madeleine Katkov, surveyed all the existing plastered walls for evidence of wall paintings which resulted in the discoveries mentioned earlier on pages 94 to 97. It was found that the whole of the south wall of the church had been re-plastered in relatively modern times, in the 18th or 19th centuries, so there was no possibility of there being any paintings left on that wall. The fragments that were discovered on the north wall were incomplete because the plaster on that wall was quite unstable and had clearly already been repaired in a number of places, resulting for example in the gaps in the large text inscription. After the completion of the survey, and the protection and stabilization of the newly discovered paintings, several areas of plaster on the north wall were removed as they were unsafe.

Throughout the church the stonework, which had been painted with white emulsion paint during the

Fig 163. Steam cleaning the white emulsion paint off the stonework

20th century, was stripped of the emulsion using a steam cleaning process, Fig 163. In the chancel arch this revealed several holes which had once held the support frame for the tympanum of the medieval rood screen and which had been filled with plaster when the screen was removed. One of these holes can now be seen towards the top of the arch. The cleaning also revealed some pieces of wood from the old screen which are still in situ on the north side of the arch. There are also some faint remains of medieval paint on the lower column of the arch on the south side, Fig 164.

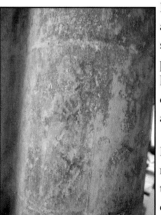

During the cleaning and preparation of the south arcade, prior to plastering, an oak lintel, Fig 165, was rediscovered in the wall above the small eastern

Fig 164. The remains of medieval decoration on the south pillar of the chancel arch

arch of the arcade, which had been noted by the Oxford Architectural and Historical Society during a visit on 22nd May 1886 as being part of the medieval doorway to the rood loft. After recording this lintel was plastered over.

Fig 165. The oak lintel of the medieval doorway onto the rood loft

The picture below of St. John the Baptist Church in Frome, Somerset, shows how our rood loft might have looked with the doorway in the south arcade.

Fig 166. Rood, screen and loft in St. John the Baptist church in Frome

In the eaves of the nave roof above the south door, a hobnailed boot was discovered, Fig 167. It is believed that this was placed there deliberately by the workmen involved in the last major refurbishment of the church in 1883 and was returned to its hiding place with a new descriptive plaque when the work in the roof was completed in March 2016.

Fig 167. The Victorian hobnailed boot

The south porch was also re-plastered and redecorated, with a new stone floor and seating. New wrought iron gates, Fig 168, depicting the Tree of Life, have been made by eminent local Master Blacksmith Michael Jacques at his workshops in the village, and the glass in the new oak doors to the church from the porch are etched with the same design. The light pendant in the porch, and all the other pendants in the church have also been made by Michael Jacques and his apprentices, Fig 169.

The early 20th century vestry partitions were removed and the painted wooden boards of the Lord's Prayer, Creed and Ten Commandments were cleaned and conserved and have been re-hung on the wall of the south aisle. The other charity boards were also refurbished and have been

Fig 168. The Tree of Life gates made by Michael Jacques

Fig 169. Michael Jacques and his apprentice working on the light pendants

Fig 170. The new digital organ console and choir stalls in the chancel

re-hung on the north and west walls of the north aisle. Other wooden furniture, altar rails, pulpit, lecterns, pews and tables were all cleaned, repaired where necessary and refurbished.

The font was removed and the white emulsion paint cleaned off it. The lower 19th century concrete pedestal was removed and the font replaced on its original stone pedestal.

The pipe organ, which was beyond economical repair, was removed and a new digital organ has been installed with the console in the chancel to the same design as the new choir stalls, Fig 170.

Externally, the tower and part of the south side of the church were scaffolded to assist in the repair of the external stonework. This included work on the south parapet, the arch of the south west window, the arch of the priest's door in the chancel, and many other replacements of worn and eroded stones. The bell louvres of the tower were all replaced with new oak louvres.

New oak cupboards have been commissioned and built along the south and west sides of the nave to house the controls of the new sound, lighting and heating systems, as well as the altar frontals, candles, and other equipment needed for the regular services in the church.

Before and during the project a photographic record of the building and works was made, from which the small selection of photos in this report are taken. They were also used to keep the village informed of progress on the project through displays in the window of the Post Office and in regular monthly reports in the village LINK magazine. Additionally, open days were held when the public were encouraged to visit the church to see the progress for themselves. Students from Chalgrove Primary School were among those who visited and they were given a special demonstration of stone carving by the Master Mason, Fig 171.

Fig 171. The Master Mason demonstrates his craft to the students from the Primary School

Fig 172. The Syon Cope now in the V & A Museum, London. This 14thC cope, embroidered with *opus anglicanum*, has several of the images which we have in our wall paintings including Saints Peter and Paul and the funeral of the Virgin Mary. © Victoria and Albert Museum, London

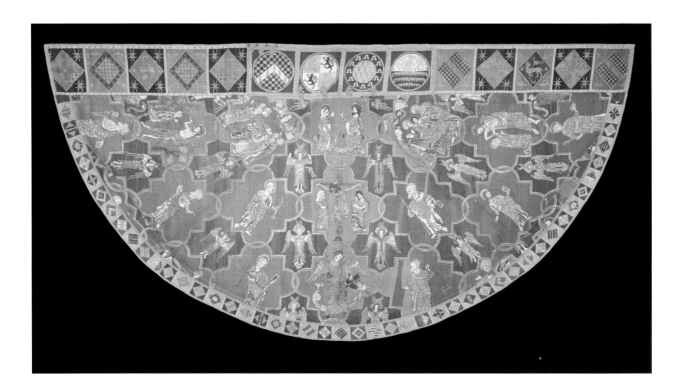

Fig 173. The carved ivory Diptych by the Master of Kremsmunster, now in the Staatliche Museum in Berlin.

Fig 174. The Soissons Diptych. Scenes from The Passion of Christ; ivory, painted and gilt; French (Paris); late 13th century. © Victoria and Albert Museum, London

Fig 175. The left hand side of an English carved ivory diptych, now in the British Museum

Note in the top picture of the Annunciation how the dove of the Holy Spirit is close to the Virgin Mary's head.

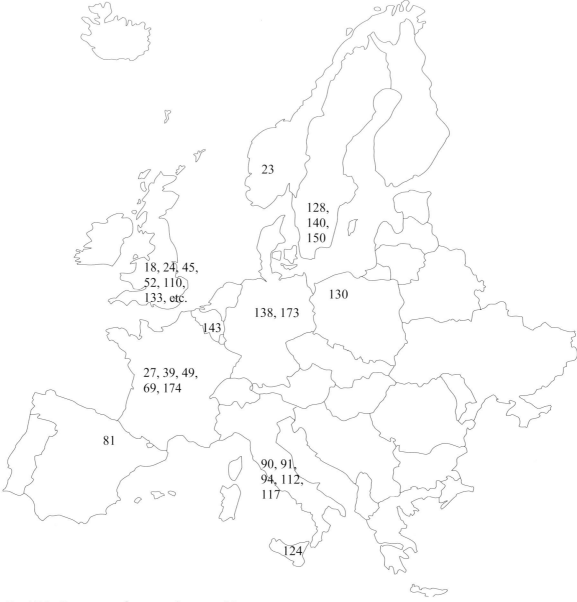

23

128,
140,
150

18, 24, 45,
52, 110,
133, etc.

130

138, 173

143

27, 39, 49,
69, 174

81

90, 91,
94, 112,
117

124

Fig 176. Countries of origin of some of the
items illustrated in this guide. The
numbers relate to figure numbers

REFERENCES AND FURTHER READING

A Collection of Articles, Injunctions, Canons, Orders, Ordinances, and Constitutions Ecclesiastical; With other Publick Records of the Church of England. Printed for Robert Pawlet, at the Bible in Chancery Lane, near Fleet Street, 1675.

A Study of the wall paintings in the chancel of St. Mary's, Chalgrove, A Dissertation submitted towards the Degree of Master of Arts in Medieval Studies. S T J Maynard, Centre for Medieval Studies, University of York, 1986.

Three Virgins, Two Widows and a Donor: who sponsored the Chalgrove church paintings?, R W Heath-Whyte, pp 44 to 65, Oxfordshire Local History, Volume 9 no. 4, Winter 2013-14, Oxford (can be downloaded from www.olha.org.uk)

On Mural Paintings in Chalgrove Church, Oxfordshire. W Burges, Archaeologia Volume xxxviii, pp 431-8, 1860.

The Golden Legend, Readings on the Saints. Jacobus de Voragine, translated by W G Ryan, Princeton University Press, 1993

The Apocryphal New Testament. Translated by M R James, Oxford University Press, Reprinted 1989.

Ancient traditions of the Virgin Mary's dormition and assumption, S J Shoemaker, Oxford University Press, 2002

A Survey of Manuscripts illuminated in the British Isles. Volume Five. Gothic Manuscripts [I] 1285-1385, Professor Lucy Freeman Sandler, Harvey Miller Publishers, Oxford University Press, 1986.

English Wall-paintings of the Fourteenth Century. E W Tristram, Routledge & Paul, London, 1955.

Medieval Wall Paintings. E Clive Rouse, Shire Publications Ltd, 1991.

Medieval Craftsmen – Painters. Paul Binski, British Museum Press, 1991

The Stripping of the Altars. Eamon Duffy, Yale University Press, 1992

Thomas Cranmer. Diarmaid MacCulloch, Yale University Press, 1996

Age of Chivalry, Art in Plantagenet England 1200-1400, Ed J Alexander & P Binski. London, Royal Academy of Arts 1987

Medieval Wall Paintings in English and Welsh Churches, R Rosewell, Woodbridge, The Boydell Press, 2008

Stained Glass in England during the Middle Ages, R Marks, Toronto, University of Toronto Press, 1993

Image and Devotion in Late Medieval England, R Marks, Stroud, Sutton Publishing Ltd, 2004

She-Wolves: The Women who ruled England before Elizabeth, H Castor, London, Faber, 2010

Edward II: The Unconventional King, K Warner, Stroud, Amberley Publishing, 2014

A Little History of the English Country Church, R Strong, London, Jonathan Cape, 2007

The Virgin's Girdle, G Lessanutti, Australia, 2012

Mother of God, M Rubin, London, Penguin, 2010

Giotto, The Scrovegni Chapel in Padua, A M Spiazzi, Milan, Skira Editore S.p.A., 2004

The Altarpiece from Jonsberg, E Hoglund, Stockholm, Statens Historiska Museum, 1995

El Ciclo de la Dormicion en el Claustro de la Catedral de Pamplona, S Hidalgo Sanchez, pp 145 to 176, Revue Mabillon, 2011

Oxfordshire, J Steane, London, Pimlico, 1996

COPYRIGHT PERMISSIONS AND PHOTOGRAPHIC CREDITS